Windows 2000 Directory Services Administration

Exam Notes

MCSE:
Windows® 2000 Directory Services Administration

Exam Notes™

Quentin Docter
with Anil Desai
and James Chellis

San Francisco • Paris • Düsseldorf • Soest • London

SYBEX

Associate Publisher: Neil Edde
Contracts and Licensing Manager: Kristine O'Callaghan
Acquisitions Editors: Dann McDorman and Brenda Frink
Developmental Editor: Bonnie Bills
Editor: Joe Webb
Production Editor: Edith Kaneshiro
Technical Editor: Michael Chacon
Book Designer: Bill Gibson
Electronic Publishing Specialists: Judy Fung and Jill Niles
Proofreaders: Andrea Fox, Amey Garber, and Nancy Riddiough
Indexer: Matthew Spence
Cover Designer: Archer Design
Cover Illustrator/Photographer: Natural Selection

Library of Congress Card Number: 00-106463

ISBN: 0-7821-2762-2

Manufactured in the United States of America

10 9 8 7 6 5 4 3 2 1

To Kara,
aishiteru

Acknowledgments

There are so many people involved in the production of a book. I never realized how complicated this whole process was. I would like to thank the following list of people, only in the order of which I think of them:

Kara, thank you for everything. I could think of a page of stuff to thank you for, but will limit the list to just one thing for now: thank you for your unconditional love and support. Kevin, thanks for getting my foot in the door. Neil Edde, thanks for not taking my foot off with that door. Bonnie Bills, thank you for pointing me in the right direction on multiple occasions. Edith Kaneshiro, thanks for your guidance on the whole project. Joe Webb, thanks for the fine-toothed comb. You made this book much better. Michael Chacon, thanks for the tech edit. Amey Garber, Andrea Fox, and Nancy Riddiough, thanks for doing a great job of proofreading the book. Dann McDorman and Brenda Frink, thank you both for your help. Judy Fung and Jill Niles, thanks for putting the finishing touches on the pages. Scott, thanks for keeping me sane. You need to stop hooking your drives though. The Fredericks: Eron, Lisa, Jon, James, and Evan. You are good people and great friends, Kara and I miss you. Rob and Amy, you're such a cute couple. Not to mention incredibly good friends too. My parents; where would I be without them? Grandpa Joe, thanks for teaching me about some of the most important things in life: Golf, chess, and computers. You taught me so much more about life as well. Judy Timmins and Loren Johnson, you both greatly improved my writing, although many times it nearly killed me. Danny Elfman, you have no idea who I am, but thanks for making great music. All of my students, past and present: Thanks for asking the tough questions I hated to answer. Those questions made me learn more, even if I didn't want to. I am sure there are people I neglected to mention. It was not intentional I assure you. Thank you.

—*Quentin Docter*

Contents

Introduction

If you've purchased this book, you are probably chasing the Microsoft Windows 2000 MCSE. This is a great goal, and also a great career builder. Glance through any newspaper, and you'll find employment opportunities for people with this certification. The ads exist because finding qualified employees is a challenge in today's market. The certification means you know something about the product; but more important, it means you have the ability, determination, and focus to learn—the greatest skill any employee can have!

You've probably also heard all the rumors about how hard the Microsoft tests are—believe us, the rumors are true! Microsoft has designed a series of exams that truly test your knowledge of their products. Each test not only covers the materials presented in a particular class; each also covers the prerequisite knowledge for that course. This means two things for you—that first test can be a real hurdle and each test *should* get easier since you've studied the basics over and over.

This book has been developed in alliance with Microsoft Corporation to give you the knowledge and skills you need to prepare for one of the key exams of the MCSE certification program: Exam 70-217: Implementing and Administering a Microsoft Windows 2000 Directory Services Infrastructure. Reviewed and approved by Microsoft, this book provides a solid introduction to Microsoft networking technologies and will help you on your way to MCSE certification.

Is This Book for You?

The MCSE Exam Notes books were designed to be succinct, portable exam-review guides that can be used either in conjunction with a more complete study program (book, CBT courseware, classroom/lab environment) or as an exam review for those who don't feel the need for more extensive test preparation. It isn't our goal to "give the answers away," but rather to identify those topics on which you can expect to be tested and to provide sufficient coverage of these topics.

Perhaps you've been working with Microsoft networking technologies for years now. The thought of paying big money for a specialized MCSE exam-preparation course probably doesn't sound too appealing. What can they teach you that you don't already know, right? Be careful, though. Many experienced network administrators have walked confidently into test centers only to walk sheepishly out of them after failing an MCSE exam. As they discovered, there's the Microsoft of the real world and the Microsoft of the MCSE exams. It's our goal with these Exam Notes books to show you where the two converge and where they diverge. After you've finished reading through this book, you should have a clear idea of how your understanding of the technologies involved matches up with the expectations of the MCSE test makers in Redmond.

Or perhaps you're relatively new to the world of Microsoft networking, drawn to it by the promise of challenging work and higher salaries. You've just waded through an 800-page MCSE study guide or taken a class at a local training center. Lots of information to keep track of, isn't it? Well, by organizing the Exam Notes books according to the Microsoft exam objectives, and by breaking up the information into concise, manageable pieces, we've created what we think is the handiest exam-review guide available. Throw it in your briefcase and carry it to work with you. As you read through the book, you'll be able to identify quickly those areas you know best and those that require more in-depth review.

NOTE   The goal of the Exam Notes series is to help MCSE candidates familiarize themselves with the subjects on which they can expect to be tested in the MCSE exams. For complete, in-depth coverage of the technologies and topics involved, we recommend the MCSE Study Guide series from Sybex.

How Is This Book Organized?

As mentioned above, this book is organized according to the official exam objectives list prepared by Microsoft for the Exam 70-217: Implementing and Administering a Microsoft Windows 2000 Directory Services Infrastructure. The chapters coincide with the broad objective groupings, such as Planning, Installation and Configuration, Monitoring and Optimization, and Troubleshooting. These groupings are also reflected in the organization of the MCSE exams.

Within each chapter, the individual exam objectives are addressed in turn. And in turn, the objective sections are further divided according to the type of information presented.

Critical Information

This section presents the greatest level of detail on information relevant to the objective. This is the place to start if you're unfamiliar with or uncertain about the technical issues related to the objective.

Necessary Procedures

Here you'll find instructions for procedures that require a lab computer to be completed. From installing operating systems to modifying configuration defaults, the information in these sections addresses the hands-on requirements for the MCSE exams.

NOTE   Not every objective has procedures associated with it. For such objectives, the Necessary Procedures section has been left out.

Exam Essentials

In this section, we've put together a concise list of the most crucial topics of subject areas that you'll need to comprehend fully prior to taking the MCSE exam. This section can help you identify those topics that might require more study on your part.

Key Terms and Concepts

Here we've compiled a mini-glossary of the most important terms and concepts related to the specific objective. You'll understand what all those technical words mean within the context of the related subject matter.

Sample Questions

For each objective, we've included a selection of questions similar to those you'll encounter on the actual MCSE exam. Answers and explanations are provided so you can gain some insight into the test-taking process.

How Do You Become an MCSE?

Attaining MCSE certification has always been a challenge. However, in the past, individuals could acquire detailed exam information—even most of the exam questions—from online "brain dumps" and third-party "cram" books or software products. For the new MCSE exams, this simply will not be the case.

To avoid the "paper-MCSE syndrome" (a devaluation of the MCSE certification because unqualified individuals manage to pass the exams), Microsoft has taken strong steps to protect the security and integrity of the new MCSE track. Prospective MCSEs will need to complete a course of study that provides not only detailed knowledge of a wide range of topics, but true skills derived from working with Windows 2000 and related software products.

In the new MCSE program, Microsoft is heavily emphasizing hands-on skills. Microsoft has stated that, "Nearly half of the core required exams' content demands that the candidate have troubleshooting skills acquired through hands-on experience and working knowledge."

Fortunately, if you are willing to dedicate time and effort with Windows 2000, you can prepare for the exams by using the proper tools. If you work through this book and the other books in this series, you should successfully meet the exam requirements.

Exam Requirements

Successful candidates must pass a minimum set of exams that measure technical proficiency and expertise:

- Candidates for MCSE certification must pass seven exams, including four core operating system exams, one design exam, and two electives.

- Candidates who have already passed three Windows NT 4 exams (70-067, 70-068, and 70-073) may opt to take an "accelerated" exam plus one core design exam and two electives.

NOTE   If you do not pass the accelerated exam after one attempt, you must pass the five core requirements and two electives.

The following tables show the exams a new certification candidate must pass. *All* of these exams are required:

Exam #	Title	Requirement Met
70-216	Implementing and Administering a Microsoft® Windows® 2000 Network Infrastructure	Core (Operating System)
70-210	Installing, Configuring, and Administering Microsoft® Windows® 2000 Professional	Core (Operating System)
70-215	Installing, Configuring, and Administering Microsoft® Windows® 2000 Server	Core (Operating System)
70-217	Implementing and Administering a Microsoft® Windows® 2000 Directory Services Infrastructure	Core (Operating System)

One of these exams is required:

Exam #	Title	Requirement Met
70-219	Designing a Microsoft® Windows® 2000 Directory Services Infrastructure	Core (Design)
70-220	Designing Security for a Microsoft® Windows® 2000 Network	Core (Design)
70-221	Designing a Microsoft® Windows® 2000 Network Infrastructure	Core (Design)

Two of these exams are required:

Exam #	Title	Requirement Met
70-219	Designing a Microsoft® Windows® 2000 Directory Services Infrastructure	Elective
70-220	Designing Security for a Microsoft® Windows® 2000 Network	Elective
70-221	Designing a Microsoft® Windows® 2000 Network Infrastructure	Elective
Any current MCSE elective	Exams cover topics such as Exchange Server, SQL Server, Systems Management Server, Internet Explorer Administrators Kit, and Proxy Server (new exams are added regularly)	Elective

NOTE For a more detailed description of the Microsoft certification programs, including a list of current MCSE electives, check Microsoft's Training and Services Web site at www.microsoft.com/trainingandservices.

Exam Registration

You may take the exams at any of more than 1,000 Authorized Prometric Testing Centers (APTCs) and VUE Testing Centers around the world. For the location of a testing center near you, call Sylvan Prometric at 800-755-EXAM (755-3926), or call VUE at 888-837-8616. Outside the United States and Canada, contact your local Sylvan Prometric or VUE registration center.

You should determine the number of the exam you want to take, and then register with the Sylvan Prometric or VUE registration center nearest to you. At this point, you will be asked for advance payment for the exam. The exams are $100 each. Exams must be taken within one year of payment. You can schedule exams up to six weeks in advance or as late as one working day prior to the date of the exam. You can cancel or reschedule your exam if you contact the center at least two working days prior to the exam. Same-day registration is available in some locations, subject to space availability. Where same-day registration is available, you must register a minimum of two hours before test time.

TIP You may also register for your exams online at www.sylvanprometric.com or www.vue.com.

When you schedule the exam, you will be provided with instructions regarding appointment and cancellation procedures, ID requirements, and information about the testing center location. In addition, you will receive a registration and payment confirmation letter from Sylvan Prometric or VUE.

Microsoft requires certification candidates to accept the terms of a Non-Disclosure Agreement before taking certification exams.

What Exam 70-217: Implementing and Administering a Microsoft Windows 2000 Directory Services Infrastructure Measures

This test is designed to measure your expertise about Active Directory Services. Test 70-217 also assumes you have knowledge about Windows 2000 Server and Professional, as well as the TCP/IP protocol suite.

Although the test questions will vary and possibly change over time, general areas need to be understood. Know about object management, which involves, but is not limited to, moving objects, users, and groups, and security. Know what GPOs are and what they are used for. Be comfortable with auditing. Have a thorough understanding of Windows 2000 DNS functionality and Active Directory structure.

Tips for Taking Your MCSE Exam

Here are some general tips for taking your exam successfully:

- Arrive early at the exam center so you can relax and review your study materials, particularly tables and lists of exam-related information.

- Read the questions carefully. Don't be tempted to jump to an early conclusion. Make sure you know exactly what the question is asking.

- Don't leave any unanswered questions. They count against you.

- When answering multiple-choice questions you're not sure about, use a process of elimination to get rid of the obviously incorrect questions first. This will improve your odds if you need to make an educated guess.

- Because the hard questions will eat up the most time, save them for last. You can move forward and backward through the exam.

- This test has many exhibits (pictures). It can be difficult, if not impossible, to view both the questions and the exhibit simulation on 14- and 15-inch screens usually found at the testing centers. Call around to each center and see if they have 17-inch monitors available. If they don't, perhaps you can arrange to bring in your own. Failing this, some have found it useful to quickly draw the diagram on the scratch paper provided by the testing center and use the monitor to view just the question.

- Many participants run out of time before they are able to complete the test. If you are unsure of the answer to a question, you may want to choose one of the answers, mark the question, and go on—an unanswered question does not help you. Once your time is up, you cannot go on to another question. However, you can remain on the question you are on indefinitely when the time runs out. Therefore, when you are almost out of time, go to a question you feel you can figure out—given enough time—and work until you feel you have got it (or the night security guard boots you out!).

- You are allowed to use the Windows calculator during your test. However, it may be better to memorize a table of the subnet addresses and, on the scratch paper supplied by the testing center, write it down before you start the test.

Once you have completed an exam, you will be given immediate, online notification of your pass or fail status. You will also receive a printed Examination Score Report indicating your pass or fail status and your exam results by section. (The test administrator will give you the printed score report.) Test scores are automatically forwarded to Microsoft within five working days after you take the test. You do not need to send your score to Microsoft. If you pass the exam, you will receive confirmation from Microsoft, typically within two to four weeks.

Contact Information

To find out more about Microsoft Education and Certification materials and programs, to register with Sylvan Prometric, or to get other useful information, check the following resources. Outside the United States or Canada, contact your local Microsoft office or Sylvan Prometric testing center.

Microsoft Certified Professional Program—(800) 636-7544

Call the MCPP number for information about the Microsoft Certified Professional program and exams, and to order the latest Microsoft Roadmap to Education and Certification.

Sylvan Prometric testing centers—(800) 755-EXAM

Contact Sylvan to register to take a Microsoft Certified Professional exam at any of more than 800 Sylvan Prometric testing centers around the world.

Microsoft Certification Development Team—Web: http://www.microsoft.com/trainingandservices/default.asp

Contact the Microsoft Certification Development Team through their Web site to volunteer for participation in one or more exam development phases or to report a problem with an exam. Address written correspondence to: Certification Development Team, Microsoft Education and Certification, One Microsoft Way, Redmond, WA 98052.

Microsoft TechNet Technical Information Network — (800) 344-2121

The network is an excellent resource for support professionals and system administrators. Outside the United States and Canada, call your local Microsoft subsidiary for information.

How to Contact the Author

Quentin can be reached at Qdocter@microcert.com.

How to Contact the Publisher

Sybex welcomes reader feedback on all of their titles. Visit the Sybex Web site at www.sybex.com for book updates and additional certification information. You'll also find online forms to submit comments or suggestions regarding this or any other Sybex book.

Chapter

1

Installing, Configuring, and Troubleshooting Active Directory

MICROSOFT EXAM OBJECTIVES COVERED IN THIS CHAPTER:

► **Install, configure, and troubleshoot the components of Active Directory.** *(pages 2 – 49)*

- Install Active Directory.
- Create sites.
- Create subnets.
- Create site links.
- Create site-link bridges.
- Create connection objects.
- Create global catalog servers.
- Move server objects between sites.
- Transfer operations master roles.
- Verify Active Directory installation.
- Implement an organizational unit (OU) structure.

► **Back up and restore Active Directory.** *(pages 49 – 62)*

- Perform an authoritative restore of the Active Directory.
- Recover from a system failure.

Microsoft's Active Directory technology stores information about all objects within your network environment, including hardware, software, network devices, and users. Furthermore, it increases capabilities while it decreases administration through the use of a hierarchical structure that mirrors a business's logical organization.

Proper network design begins before any implementation starts. A successful network installation often involves twice as many hours of planning than actual installation work. Designing and implementing a good organizational unit (OU) structure that maps to the network's physical and administrative needs makes that process flow. After roll-out, your network will be easier to administer and modify.

Once your network's OU structure is designed, it's time to divide the network into manageable pieces. This is where sites and subnets come in. To connect sites and subnets, and make administration easier, you can use site links, bridges, connection objects, and global catalog servers.

Keeping the network up and running maximizes company productivity. However, no matter how much preventative maintenance is done, failures do occur. For this reason, you need to be familiar with various methods of backing up and restoring the Active Directory.

Install, configure, and troubleshoot the components of Active Directory.

The success of your Active Directory implementation depends on both good planning and technical know-how. Services such as DNS are also critical to successful implementations of Active Directory.

NOTE For more information on DNS, please see Chapter 2.

Critical Information

The first and most important step in implementing any network structure is proper planning. Microsoft's Active Directory is no exception. The more complex the network is expected to be, the more critical planning becomes to a successful rollout.

Preparing for Active Directory Installation

All too often, systems and network administrators implement hardware and software without first taking the time to evaluate the prerequisites. The physical components that form the basis of the Active Directory are Windows 2000 domain controllers. Before you begin installing domain controllers to set up your Active Directory environment, you should be sure you are properly prepared.

NOTE The technical information in this chapter is based upon the assumption you will be using Microsoft's DNS (unless otherwise noted). You may choose other DNS servers when installing the Active Directory; however, you may not be able to take advantage of all the features mentioned.

Install DNS

Proper installation and configuration of DNS must be completed before installing an Active Directory domain. If it is not already installed on the system, you can install the DNS service by using the Add/Remove Programs icon in the Control Panel. DNS will be used for performing name resolution to other domain controllers or resources on your network (if any).

NOTE If you haven't yet installed DNS, you will be prompted to do so as part of the configuration of a domain controller. This provides an easy way to configure DNS with the appropriate options for the Active Directory. In a production environment, however, it can be easier to test and verify DNS server configuration before starting the Active Directory installation.

If you are using DNS servers other than Windows 2000 (such as Unix or Windows NT 4), you will most likely be required to enter the proper SRV records manually, as most current DNS servers do not support dynamic updates. While possible, the manual modification required for a static DNS is not a realistic approach for day-to-day management. Certain mixed-DNS environments can obviate manual modification, provided the non–Windows 2000 DNS servers support dynamic updates. Or, in a mixed environment, responsibility for updates can be delegated to a server that supports dynamic updates. It makes life easier, though, to utilize a straight Windows 2000 environment.

Verify the DNS Configuration

Once DNS has been installed, be sure it has been configured to allow updates. The Active Directory would then automatically add, modify, and remove resource records (RRs) to the DNS database whenever changes were made in the Active Directory. The Allow Updates option is extremely useful, as it reduces the chances for error in manual data entry and greatly reduces the effort required for administration.

Verify the File System

The file system used by an operating system is an important concern for several reasons. First, the file system can provide the ultimate level of security for all the information stored on the server. Second, the file system is responsible for managing and tracking this information. Third, file systems have certain features exclusive to the system, including support for encryption, remote file access, remote storage, disk redundancy, and disk quotas.

The Windows 2000 platform allows the use of multiple different file systems, including:

- File Allocation Table (FAT) file system

- File Allocation Table 32 (FAT32) file system

- Windows NT File System (NTFS)

- Windows NT File System (NTFS 5)

The fundamental difference between FAT and NTFS partitions is that NTFS allows for file system-level security. Support for FAT and FAT32 are mainly included in Windows 2000 for backward compatibility. Specifically, these file systems are required in order to accommodate multiple boot partitions. For example, if you wanted to configure a single computer to boot into Windows 98 and Windows 2000, you would need to have at least one FAT or FAT32 partition. Although this is a good solution for training labs and test environments, you should strongly consider using only NTFS partitions on production servers.

Windows 2000 uses an updated version of the NTFS file system called NTFS 5. Other than file system-level security, there are many benefits to using the NTFS 5 file system, including support for the following:

Disk Quotas   In order to restrict the amount of disk space for users on the network, systems administrators can establish disk quotas. By default, Windows 2000 supports disk quotas on a volume level. That is, you can restrict the amount of storage space on a single-disk volume utilized by a specific user. Third-party solutions that allow more specific quota settings are also available.

File System Encryption   One of the fundamental problems with network operating systems is that systems administrators are often given full permissions to view all files and data stored on hard disks. In some cases, this is necessary. For example, in order to perform backup, recovery, and disk-management functions, at least one user must have all permissions. Windows 2000 and NTFS 5 address the security issue by allowing for file-system encryption. Encryption essentially scrambles all data stored within files before they are written to disk. When an authorized user requests the files, they are transparently decrypted and provided. The use of encryption prevents the usability of data in case it is stolen or intercepted by an unauthorized user.

Dynamic Volumes   Protecting against disk failures is an important concern for production servers. Although earlier versions of Windows NT supported various levels of Redundant Array of Independent Disks (RAID) technology, there were shortcomings in this software-based solution. Perhaps the most significant was the requirement of server reboots in order to change RAID configurations. Some configuration changes could not be made without a complete reinstallation of the operating system. With the support for dynamic volumes in Windows 2000, systems administrators can change RAID and other disk-configuration settings without requiring a reboot or reinstallation of the server. The end result is greater protection for data, increased scalability, and increased uptime.

Mounted Drives   With the use of mounted drives, systems administrators can map a local disk drive to an NTFS 5 directory name. The mapping is useful for organizing disk space on servers and increasing manageability. By using mounted drives, you could mount the C:\Users directory to an actual physical disk. If that disk were to become full, you could copy all the files to another, larger drive, without requiring any changes to the directory path name or reconfiguration of applications.

Remote Storage   Gaining space by moving infrequently used files to tape is one way to recover disk space. However, backing up and restoring these files could be quite difficult and time consuming. You can use the Remote Storage features supported by NTFS 5 to automatically off-load seldom-used data to tape or other devices. The files remain available to users; should they request an archived file, Windows 2000 can automatically restore the file from a remote storage device.

Although the aforementioned reasons may compel you to use the NTFS 5 file system, one factor proves its use mandatory: the Active Directory data store must reside on an NTFS 5 partition. Therefore, before you begin the installation process for Active Directory, at least one NTFS partition must be available. Be sure you have a reasonable amount of disk space free, as the size of the Active Directory data store will grow as you add objects to it.

Verify Network Connectivity

Before you begin to install the Active Directory, make sure you can connect to other computers, either on your network or on the Internet.

Determine the Domain Controller Mode

When installing a Windows 2000 domain controller, you must determine if you will be supporting a *mixed-mode Active Directory* or *native-mode Active Directory*. The decision should be quite simple.

Mixed mode, the default option when installing a domain controller, is designed for allowing backward compatibility with Windows NT 4 and earlier domain models. If you need to support Windows NT domain controllers in your environment, you should choose mixed mode; however, certain Active Directory features (such as universal and nested groups) will be unavailable.

If your environment does not require Windows NT support, you can install the domain controller in native mode. Native mode allows the full functionality of the Active Directory, but it does not allow for backward compatibility.

Plan the Domain Structure

Once you verify the technical configuration of your server for the Active Directory, it's time to verify the Active Directory configuration for your organization. Besides the domain-controller mode, you should know the following information prior to beginning setup:

- The DNS name of the domain

- The NetBIOS name of the server (used by previous versions of Windows to access server resources)

- Whether or not other DNS servers are available on the network

If you will be installing additional domain controllers in your environment or will be attaching to an existing Active Directory structure, you should also have the following information:

- If this domain controller will join an existing domain, the name of that domain. You will also either require a password for an Enterprise Administrator or have someone with those permissions create a domain account before promotion.

- The name of an existing tree the new domain will join (if applicable).

- The name of a forest to which this domain will connect (if applicable).

Installing Active Directory

Installation of the Active Directory is an easy and straightforward process, assuming you have planned adequately and made the necessary decisions.

With previous versions of Windows NT Server, you had to know at installation the role of your server. Choices included making the machine a Primary Domain Controller (PDC), a Backup Domain Controller (BDC), or a member server. This was an extremely important decision—although a BDC could be promoted to a PDC, a change from domain controller to member server (or vice versa) required a complete reinstallation of the operating system.

Instead of forcing you to decide at setup whether the machine will be a domain controller, Windows 2000 allows you to promote servers after installation. At the end of the setup process, all Windows 2000 Server computers are configured as either member servers (if they are joined to a domain) or stand-alone servers (if they are part of a workgroup). The process of converting a member server to a domain controller is known as *promotion*. After installation, through the *Active Directory Installation Wizard* or with *DCPROMO* at the command line, you can quickly configure servers to be domain controllers.

Implementing Additional Domain Controllers

The Active Directory Installation Wizard has been designed to make promotion and demotion (that is, the conversion of a domain controller back to member servers or stand-alone servers) as easy as possible, without reinstalling the operating system. The Wizard also allows you to decide if the domain will participate in an existing forest or tree. Here, you can easily specify the options necessary to create new domains and complete the promotion.

Verifying Active Directory Installation

Once the Active Directory has been configured, you'll want to verify that it is properly installed. There are several good ways to do so.

Using Event Viewer

The first (and perhaps most informative) way to verify the operations of the Active Directory is to use the Windows 2000 Event Viewer to view information stored in the Windows 2000 event log. In addition to utilizing the Event Viewer to locate information about the status of events related to the Active Directory, you should make it a habit to routinely visit this area to find information about other system services and applications.

Using the Active Directory Administrative Tools

Following the promotion of a server to a domain controller, you will see various tools added to the Administrative Tools program group (see Figure 1.1). The tools, helpful for testing, are:

Active Directory Domains and Trusts   This tool is used to view and change information related to the domains in an Active Directory environment.

Active Directory Sites and Services   This tool is used for creating and letting you to manage Active Directory Sites and Services. Sites and Services allows you to map the logical network to an organization's physical network infrastructure.

Active Directory Users and Computers   User and computer management is fundamental for an Active Directory environment. The Active Directory Users and Computers tool lets you set machine- and user-specific settings across the domain.

FIGURE 1.1: Some of the many Windows 2000 Administrative Tools

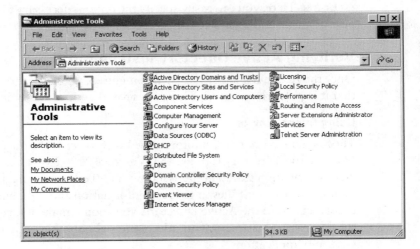

A good test of Active Directory functionality is to run the Active Directory Users and Computers tool. When you open the tool, check that the name of the domain you created appears in the list. You should also click the Domain Controllers folder to ensure that the name of your local server appears in the right-hand pane. If the names appear in the proper places, the Active Directory is present and configured.

Testing from Clients

The best test of any system is to simply verify it works the way you had intended in your environment. A good test of the Active Directory is to ascertain that clients can view and access the various resources presented by Windows 2000 domain controllers.

VERIFYING CLIENT CONNECTIVITY

Perhaps the most relevant way to test the Active Directory is by testing operations from clients. Using previous versions of Windows (such as Windows NT 4 or Windows 95/98), you should be able to see your server on the network. Earlier versions of Windows-based clients will recognize the NetBIOS name of the domain controller. Windows 2000 computers should also be able to see resources in the domain, and users can browse for resources using the My Network Places icon.

NOTE   If you are unable to see the recently promoted server on the network, it is likely due to a network-configuration error. If only one or a few clients are unable to see the machine, the problem is probably related to client-side configuration. Ensure that client computers have the appropriate TCP/IP configuration (including DNS server settings) and that they can see other computers on the network.

If the new domain controller is unavailable from any of the other client computers, verify the proper start-up of the Active Directory using the methods mentioned earlier. If the Active Directory has been started, make sure the DNS settings are correct. Finally, test network connectivity between the server and the clients by accessing the My Network Places icon.

JOINING A DOMAIN

If the Active Directory has been properly configured, clients and other servers should be able to join the domain. Clients should then be able to view Active Directory resources using the My Network Places icon. The test validates the proper functioning of the Active Directory and guarantees that you have connectivity with client computers.

Implementing an Organizational Unit (OU) Structure.

Now that Active Directory is installed, it's time to look at how an organization's business structure can be mirrored within the Active Directory through the use of *organizational units* (OUs). Because the concepts related to OUs are quite simple, some systems administrators may underestimate their importance. One of the fundamental components of a successful Active Directory installation is the proper design and deployment of OUs.

Overview of OUs

OUs are "containers" that logically group Active Directory objects, just as the name implies. OUs do not form part of the DNS namespace. They are used solely to create organization within a domain.

OUs can contain the following types of Active Directory objects:

User Objects   User objects are the fundamental *security principals* used in an Active Directory environment. A user object includes a username, a password, group-membership information, and many customizable fields that describe the user (e.g., fields for a street address, a telephone number, and other contact information).

Group Objects   Group objects arrange users to assign security permissions to resources. When managing users, the recommended practice is to place them into groups and assign permissions to the groups. This allows for flexible management and obviates the need for systems administrators to set permissions for individual users.

Computer Objects   Computer objects represent workstations that are part of the Active Directory domain. Every computer within a domain shares the same security database, including user and group information. Computer objects are useful for managing security permissions and enforcing *Group Policy* restrictions.

Shared Folders   One of the fundamental functions of servers is to make resources available to users. Often, shared folders are used to give logical names to specific collections of files. For example, you might create shared folders for common applications, user data, and shared public files. Shared folders can be created and managed within the Active Directory.

Other Organizational Units   Perhaps the most useful feature of OUs is they can contain *other* OUs. You can therefore hierarchically group resources and other objects in accordance with business practices. The OU structure is extremely flexible and can easily be rearranged to reflect business reorganizations.

The Purpose and Benefits of OUs

Before diving into the details of OUs, it is very important to understand how OUs, users, and groups interact. Although OUs are containers, they are not groups in the classical sense. That is, they do not contain users, groups, or computers and are not used per se for assigning security permissions. Stated another way, the user accounts, computer accounts, and group accounts contained in OUs are considered security principals, while OUs themselves are not.

OUs do not take the place of standard user and group permissions. After assigning users to groups and placing groups into OUs, security permissions still need to be set.

An organizational unit contains objects only from within the domain in which it resides. OUs are the lowest level for setting Group Policies and other administrative settings.

The many benefits to using OUs throughout your network environment include:

- OUs are the smallest unit to which you can assign permissions.

- The OU structure can be easily changed, and OU structure is more flexible than domain structure.

- The OU structure can support many different levels of hierarchy.

- Child objects can inherit OU settings.

- You can set Group Policy settings on OUs.

- Administration of OUs and the objects within them can be easily delegated to the appropriate users and groups.

Logical Grouping of Resources

Hierarchical groups are quite intuitive and widely used in most businesses. A typical manufacturing business might divide its operations into different departments, such as:

- Sales
- Marketing
- Engineering
- Research and Development
- Support
- Information Technology (IT)

Each of these departments usually has its own goals and missions. In order to make the business competitive, individuals within each of the departments will be assigned roles. Some roles might be:

- Managers
- Clerical Staff
- Technical Staff
- Planners

Each of these roles usually entails specific job responsibilities. For example, managers should be responsible for providing direction to general staff members. Note that the very nature of these roles suggests employees may fill many different positions. That is, you might be a Manager in one department and a member of the Technical Staff in another. In the modern workplace, such a situation is quite common.

How does the preceding information help in planning for OUs? First and foremost, the structure of OUs within a given network environment should map well to the needs of the business, such as outlined for the typical manufacturing business. You will need to focus on the administrative and logical structure of the organization, as well as its technical needs.

What's in a name? When it comes to designing the Active Directory, the answer is plenty! When naming OUs for your organization, you should keep several considerations in mind:

Keep it simple.   The purpose of OUs is to make administration and usage of resources easy. Therefore, it's always a good idea to keep the names of your objects simple and descriptive. Sometimes, finding a balance between the two can be a challenge. For example, although a printer name like "The LaserJet located near Bob's Cube" might seem descriptive, it is certainly difficult to type. Imagine the naming changes that might be required if Bob moves (or leaves the company)!

Pay attention to limitations.   The maximum length for the name of an OU is 65 characters. In most cases, this should be adequate. Remember, the name of an OU object does not have to uniquely describe it, because the OU will generally be referenced as part of the overall hierarchy.

Pay attention to the hierarchical consistency.   The fundamental basis of an OU structure is adherence to a hierarchy. From a design standpoint, this means you cannot have two OUs with the same name at the same level. However, you can have OUs with the same name at different levels. For example, you could create a Corporate OU within both the North America OU and the South America OU, because the fully qualified name includes information about the hierarchy. When an administrator tries to access resources in the Corporate OU, they must specify *which* Corporate OU. Furthermore, users and administrators will depend on the hierarchy of OUs within the domain, so make sure it remains logically consistent. If, for example, you create a North American OU, the Canada OU should logically fit under it. If you decide you want to separate them into different containers, other names might be more appropriate. For example, North America could be changed to U.S.

OU Inheritance

When OUs are rearranged within the structure of the Active Directory, several settings may be changed. You must pay careful attention to changes in security permissions and other configuration options when moving and reorganizing OUs. By default, OUs will inherit the permissions of their new parent container when moved.

NOTE When using the built-in tools provided with Windows 2000 and the Active Directory, you can only move or copy OUs within the same domain.

Delegation of Administrative Control

Delegation is when a higher security authority gives permissions to another. As a real-world example, assume that you are the Director of IT for a large organization. Instead of doing all of the work yourself (which would result in a very long work day!), you would probably assign roles and responsibilities to other individuals. For example, you might make one systems administrator responsible for all operations within the Sales domain and another responsible for the Engineering domain. Likewise, you could assign the permissions for managing all printers and print queues within the organization to one individual, while allowing another to manage all security permissions for users and groups.

A good general rule of thumb is to provide users and administrators the minimum permissions they require to do their jobs. Accidental, malicious, and otherwise unwanted changes would then not occur.

In the world of the Active Directory, delegation is used to define the permissions for administrators of OUs. When delegating, it is crucial to understand parent-child relationships. You can choose to allow child containers to automatically inherit the permissions set on parent containers. For example, if the North America division of your organization contains 12 other OUs, you could delegate permissions to all of them by placing security permissions on the North America division.

Inheritance—when child objects take on permissions of the parent—can be overridden if your business rules are not conducive to this feature. Inheritance can greatly ease administration, especially in larger organizations, but underscores the need for proper OU planning.

Application of Group Policy

One of the major design goals for the Windows 2000 platform (and specifically, the Active Directory) was manageability. Although the broad range of features and functionality provided by the operating system is nice, being able to control what users can do on their systems is more important.

That's where Group Policies come in. Group Policies are collections of permissions that can be applied to objects within the Active Directory. Specifically, Group Policy settings are assigned at the OU level and can apply to user accounts, computer accounts, and groups. Examples of settings that a systems administrator can make using Group Policies include:

- Restricting access to the Start menu
- Disallowing the use of the Control Panel
- Limiting choices for display and desktop settings

Group Policies are further covered in Chapter 3.

Creating OUs

Through the use of the Active Directory Users and Groups administrative tool, you can quickly and easily add, move, and change OUs. This graphical tool makes it easy to visualize and create the various levels of hierarchy required within an organization.

Note that OU structures can be designed in several different ways. For example, you could group all offices located in the United States within a U.S. OU. However, due to the size of the offices, you might choose to place them at the same level as the Canada and Mexico OUs, to prevent an unnecessarily deep OU hierarchy.

Managing OUs

Managing network environments would be challenging enough if things rarely changed. However, in the real world, business units, departments, and employee roles change frequently. Fortunately, changing the structure of OUs within a domain is a relatively simple process.

Deleting, Moving, and Renaming OUs

When you delete an OU, the objects contained within it are deleted as well.

Moving OUs is extremely simple. Here are some examples of why you may want to move an OU:

- The Research and Engineering departments have been combined together to form a department known as Research and Development (RD).

- The Training department has been moved from under the Technical department to the Human Resources department.

- The Marketing department has been moved from the New York office to the Chicago office.

Renaming OUs does not change any of the other properties of the OU.

Administering Properties of OUs

OUs have several settings that can be modified. To modify the properties of an OU using the Active Directory Users and Computers administrative tool, you can right-click the name of any OU and select Properties.

In any organization, it's useful to know who is responsible for the management of an OU. This information can be set on the Managed By tab (see Figure 1.2). The information specified in this tab is very convenient, as it will automatically pull the contact information from a user record. You should consider always having a contact for each OU within your organization so users and other systems administrators will know whom to contact should the need for changes arise.

FIGURE 1.2: Setting OU Managed By properties

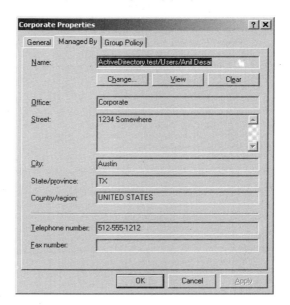

Delegating Control of OUs

In simple environments, one or a few systems administrators may be responsible for managing all of the settings within the Active Directory. Typically, a systems administrator would be responsible for objects within only a few OUs in an Active Directory domain. Or, one systems administrator could be responsible for managing user and group objects while another would be responsible for managing file and print services.

The Active Directory Users and Computers tool provides a Delegation of Control Wizard (see Figure 1.3), a quick and easy method for ensuring that specific users receive only the permissions they require.

FIGURE 1.3: The Delegation of Control Wizard

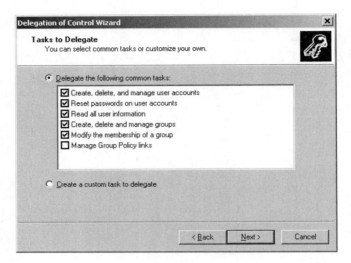

Although the common tasks available through the Wizard will be sufficient for many delegation operations, in some cases you may want more control. Toward that end, the Delegation of Control Wizard allows the assignment of custom tasks.

Troubleshooting OUs

The most common problems with OU configuration are related to the OU structure. When troubleshooting OUs, pay careful attention to the following factors:

Inheritance By default, Group Policy and other settings are transferred automatically from parent OUs to child OUs and objects. Even if a particular OU is not assigned a specific a set of permissions, objects within that OU might still get them from that OU's parent objects.

Delegation of Administration If the wrong user accounts or groups are allowed to perform specific tasks on OUs, you might be violating your company's security policy. Be sure to verify the delegations you have made at each OU level.

Organizational Issues   Sometimes, business practices may not easily map to the structure of the Active Directory. A few misplaced OUs, user accounts, computer accounts, or groups can make administration difficult or inaccurate. In many cases, it might be beneficial to rearrange the OU structure to accommodate any changes in the business organization. In others, it might make more sense to change business processes.

If you make it a practice to regularly consider each of these issues when troubleshooting problems with OUs, you will be much less likely to make errors in the Active Directory configuration.

Domain Trees and Forests

Windows 2000 Active Directory is scalable to any size network; you can create multiple domains. Regardless of the number of domains in your environment, you always have a tree and a forest. This might come as a surprise to those of you who generally think of domain trees and forests in terms of multiple domains. However, when you install the first domain in an Active Directory environment, that domain automatically creates a new forest and a new tree. Of course, there are no other domains that form the tree or forest.

A domain tree contains one or more domains that share a contiguous namespace. That is, all domains within a given tree are linked together by a common root domain. For example, all of the following domains make up a single contiguous namespace (and can therefore be combined together to form a single domain tree):

- `sales.company.com`
- `it.company.com`
- `company.com`
- `northamerica.sales.company.com`

In some cases you may want to combine Active Directory domains that do not share a contiguous namespace. In other words, you want to merge two or more trees together. Such a structure is known as a forest. The following domains do not share a contiguous namespace:

- `sales.company1.com`
- `sales.company2.com`
- `company3.com`

In order to manage the relationship between these domains, you would need to create three separate domain trees (one for each domain) and then combine them into a forest.

If you're unfamiliar with the use of multiple domains, you might be wondering, "Why bother to join domains together into a tree or forest?" Good question! The main reason is to ease the sharing of resources.

All domains within a single Active Directory forest have several features in common, described as follows.

Schema

The schema is the Active Directory structure that defines how the information within the data store will be organized. In order for the information stored on various domain controllers to remain compatible, all domain controllers within the entire Active Directory environment must share the same schema. For example, if you added a field for an employee's benefits plan number, all domain controllers throughout the environment would need to recognize this type of information before it could be shared between them.

Global Catalog

One of the problems associated with working in large network environments is that sharing information across multiple domains can be costly in terms of network and server resources. The Active Directory schema allows for a standardized set of information to be stored. However, one potential problem is realized when users try to search for resources across many domains. Generally, there is not one specific repository of information regarding available resources.

Fortunately, the Active Directory has a better solution: the *Global Catalog* (GC). The GC is a repository of subset information of all objects within *all* Active Directory domains within a forest. Systems administrators can determine what types of information should be added to the defaults in the GC. Generally, the decision is to store commonly used information, such as a list of all of the printers, users, groups, and computers. Specific domain controllers can be configured to carry a copy of the GC.

Configuration Information

There are some roles and functions that must be managed for the entire forest. When dealing with multiple domains, you must configure certain domain controllers to perform functions for the entire Active Directory environment.

Managing Multiple Domains

You can easily manage most of the operations that must occur *between* domains by using the Active Directory Domains and Trusts administrative tool. If, on the other hand, you want to configure settings *within* a domain, you should use the Active Directory Users and Computers tool.

Managing Single Master Operations

For the most part, the Active Directory functions in what is known as *multimaster replication*. That is, every domain controller within the environment contains a copy of the Active Directory data store that is both readable and writeable. This works well for most types of information. For example, if you want to modify the password of a user, you can easily do this on *any* of the domain controllers within a domain. The change will then be automatically propagated to the other domain controllers.

There are, however, some functions not managed in a multimaster fashion, known as FSMOs or flexible single-master operations. Single-master operations must be performed on specially designated machines within the Active Directory forest. There are five main single-master functions. Two single-master functions apply to an entire Active Directory forest:

Schema Master   All domain controllers within a single Active Directory environment must share the same schema, for consistency of information. Developers and systems administrators can, however, modify the Active Directory schema by adding custom information. An example might be adding a field to employee information that specifies a user's favorite color. These types of changes must be performed on the domain controller that serves as the *Schema Master* for the environment. The Schema Master is then responsible for propagating all changes to all other domain controllers within the forest.

Domain Naming Master   The purpose of the *Domain Naming Master* is to keep track of all the domains within an Active Directory forest. This domain controller is accessed whenever new domains are added to a tree or forest.

Three single-master functions apply to each domain. *Within* each domain, at least one domain controller must fulfill each of the following roles:

Relative ID (RID) Master   It is extremely important that every object within the Active Directory be assigned a unique identifier so they are distinguishable. For example, if you have two OUs named IT that reside in different domains, there must be some way to easily differentiate the two objects. Furthermore, if you delete one of the IT OUs and then later re-create it, the system must be able to determine it is not the same object as the other IT OU. The unique identifier for each object is made up of a domain identifier and a relative identifier. RIDs are used for managing security information and authenticating users. The *Relative ID (RID) Master* is responsible for creating these identifiers within a domain whenever new Active Directory objects are created.

PDC Emulator Master   Within a domain, the *Primary Domain Controller (PDC) Emulator* is responsible for maintaining backward compatibility with Windows NT domain controllers. When running in mixed-mode domains, the PDC Emulator is able to process authentication requests and serve as a PDC with Windows NT Backup Domain Controllers (BDCs). When running in native-mode domains (which do not support the use of pre-Windows 2000 domain controllers), the *PDC Emulator Master* serves as the default domain controller to process authentication requests if another domain controller is unable to do so. The PDC Emulator Master will also receive preferential treatment whenever domain security changes are made.

Infrastructure Master   Whenever a user is added to or removed from a group, all domain controllers must be made aware of this change. The role of the *Infrastructure Master* is to ascertain that group membership information stays synchronized within an Active Directory domain.

Global Catalog Servers

One of the best features of a distributed-directory service like the Active Directory is different pieces of information can be stored throughout an organization. For example, a domain in Japan might store a list of users who operate within a company's Asian Operations business unit while one in New York would contain a list of users who operate within its North American Operations business unit. This architecture allows systems administrators to place the most frequently accessed information on domain controllers in different domains, thereby reducing disk-space requirements and replication traffic.

A problem exists, however, involving querying information stored within the Active Directory. What would happen, for example, if a user wanted a list of all printers available in all domains within the Active Directory forest? In this case, the search would normally require information from at least one domain controller in each of the domains within the environment. Some of these domain controllers may be located across slow network links or may have unreliable connections. The user would have an extremely long wait for the results of the query.

The Active Directory has a mechanism that speeds up such searches. Any number of domain controllers can be configured to host a copy of the Global Catalog. The Global Catalog contains all schema information and a subset of the attributes of all domains within the Active Directory environment. Although a default set of information is normally included with the Global Catalog, systems administrators can add additional information to this data store. Servers that contain a copy of the Global Catalog are known as *Global Catalog servers*. Whenever a user executes a query that requires information from multiple domains, they need only contact their nearest Global Catalog server for this information. Similarly, when users are required to authenticate across domains, they will not have to wait for a response from a domain controller located across the world.

Active Directory Site Concepts

Active Directory domains, organizational units, users, groups, and computers are all designed to map to administrative requirements of a business. But the Active Directory can also map to an organization's *physical* requirements. Specifically, you must consider network connectivity between sites and the flow of information between *domain controllers* under less than ideal conditions. These constraints will determine how domain controllers can work together to ensure that the objects within the Active Directory remain synchronized, no matter how large and geographically dispersed the network is.

Through the use of the Active Directory Sites and Services administrative tool, you can quickly and easily create the components of an Active Directory replication topology, including the creation of objects called *sites*, the placement of servers in sites, and the creation of connections between sites. Once you have configured *Active Directory replication* to fit your current network environment, you can sit back while the Active Directory makes sure information remains consistent across domain controllers. Through the use of sites, you will be able to leverage your network infrastructure to best support Windows 2000 and the Active Directory.

Stated simply, a *site* is a collection of well-connected computers. There is no specified relationship between Active Directory domains and Active Directory sites. An Active Directory site can contain many domains. Alternatively, a single Active Directory domain can span multiple sites.

There are two main reasons to use Active Directory sites: for service requests and for replication.

Service Requests

Clients often require the network services of a domain controller. One of the most common reasons is they need the domain controller to perform network authentication. Through the use of Active Directory sites, clients can easily connect to the domain controller located closest to them. They thus avoid many of the inefficiencies associated with connecting to distant domain controllers or those located on the other side of a slow network connection. Connecting to the nearest domain controller reduces network costs and increases performance. In order for this to work well, you must define which services are available at specific sites.

Replication

Active Directory replication is designed to certify that the information stored on domain controllers remains synchronized. However, in environments with many domains and domain controllers, there are multiple paths of communication, which makes synchronization more complicated. One method of transferring updates and other changes to the Active Directory would be for all of the servers to communicate directly with each other as soon as a change occurs. This is not ideal because it places high requirements on network bandwidth, and many networks use slower and more costly WAN links. How can you efficiently solve this problem?

Through the use of sites, the Active Directory automatically determines the best methods for performing replication operations. Sites take into account an organization's network infrastructure and are used by the Active Directory to determine the most efficient method for synchronizing information between domain controllers. Systems administrators can make their physical network design map to logical Active Directory objects. Based on the creation and configuration of these objects, the Active Directory service can then manage replication traffic in an efficient way.

Whenever a change is made to the Active Directory database on a domain controller, the change is given a logical sequence number. The domain controller can then propagate these changes to other domain controllers based on replication settings. In the event that the same setting (such as a user's last name) has been changed on two different domain controllers (before replication can take place), these sequence numbers are used to resolve the conflict.

NOTE Directory Replication is fully covered in Chapter 4.

Sites and Subnets

Here's a quick overview of the various Active Directory objects that are related to physical network topology:

Subnets A *subnet* is a partition of a network. Subnets are usually connected through the use of routers and other network devices. All the computers located on a given subnet are generally well connected.

Sites An Active Directory site is a logical object that can contain servers and other objects related to Active Directory replication. Specifically, a site is a grouping of related subnets. Sites are created to match the physical network structure of an organization.

Site Links *Site links* are created to define the types of connections available between the components of a site. Site links can reflect a relative cost for a network connection and the bandwidth available for communications.

Each of these components works together in determining how information is used to replicate data between domain controllers. Overall, the use of sites allows you to control the behavior of the Active Directory replication.

Creating Sites

The primary method for creating and managing Active Directory replication components is to utilize the Active Directory Sites and Services tool. Using this administrative component, you can graphically create and manage sites in much the same way as you create and manage OUs.

Creating Subnets

Once you have created the sites that map to your network topology, it's time to define the subnets that belong with the site.

WARNING   A solid understanding of how TCP/IP and subnetting work is critical to the successful implementation of Active Directory among multiple sites.

Subnets are based on TCP/IP address information and take the form of a TCP/IP address and a subnet mask. For example, the TCP/IP address may be 10.120.0.0, and the subnet mask may be 255.255.0.0. This information specifies that all TCP/IP addresses that begin with the first two octets are part of the same TCP/IP subnet. All of the following TCP/IP addresses would be within this subnet:

- 10.120.1.5
- 10.120.100.17
- 10.120.120.120

The Active Directory Sites and Services tool expresses these subnets in a somewhat different notation. It uses the provided subnet address and appends a slash followed by the number of bits in the subnet mask. In the example above, the subnet would be defined as 10.120.0.0/16.

Site Links and Site-Link Bridges

The overall topology of intersite replication is based on the use of site links and site link bridges. *Site links* are logical connections that define a path between two Active Directory sites. Site links can include several descriptive elements that define their network characteristics. *Site-link bridges* are used to connect site links together so that the relationship can be transitive.

Both of these logical connections are used by the Active Directory services to determine how information should be synchronized between domain controllers in remote sites. How is this information used? The Knowledge Consistency Checker (KCC) forms a replication topology based on the site topology created. KCC determines the best way to replicate information within and between sites.

When creating site links for your environment, you'll need to consider the factors discussed next.

Transport

You can choose to use either IP or SMTP for transferring information over a site link. The main determination will be based on your network infrastructure and the reliability of connections between sites. SMTP is usually used for sites that have intermittent connections, such as dial-up.

Cost

Multiple site links can be created between sites. Site links can be assigned a cost value based on the type of connection. The systems administrator determines the cost value, and the relative costs of site links are then used to determine the optimal path for replication. The lower the cost, the more likely the link is to be used for replication.

For example, a company may primarily use a T1 link between branch offices, but it may also use a slower dial-up Integrated Services Digital Network (ISDN) connection for redundancy (in case the T1 fails). In this example, a systems administrator may assign a cost of 25 to the T1 line and a cost of 100 to the ISDN line so that the more reliable and higher-bandwidth T1 connection is used whenever available.

Schedule

Once you've determined how and through which connection replication will take place, determine *when* information should be replicated. Replication requires network resources and occupies bandwidth. Therefore, you will need to balance the need for consistent directory information with the need to conserve bandwidth. For example, if you decide it's reasonable to have a lag time of six hours between an update at one site and its replication to all others, you might schedule replication to occur once in the morning, once during the lunch hour, and more frequently after normal work hours.

Connection Objects

Generally, it is a good practice to allow the Active Directory's replication mechanisms to automatically schedule and manage replication functions. In some cases, however, you may want to have additional control over replication. Perhaps you want to replicate changes on demand when you create new accounts. Or, you may want to specify a custom schedule for certain servers.

You can set up these different types of replication schedules through the use of connection objects. Connection objects can be created with the Active Directory Sites and Services tool by expanding a server object, right-clicking the NTDS (Windows NT Directory Services) Settings object, and selecting New ➤ Connections.

Through the properties of the Connection object, you can specify for replication the type of transport (RPC, IP, or SMTP), the schedule, and the domain controllers that will participate (see Figure 1.4). Additionally, you will have the ability to right-click the Connection object and select Replicate Now.

FIGURE 1.4: Viewing the properties of a Connection object

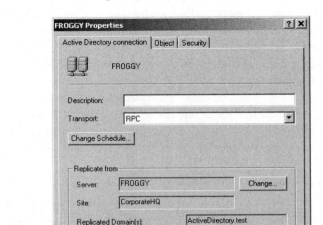

Moving Server Objects between Sites

Using the Active Directory Sites and Services tool, you can easily move servers between sites. To do this, just right-click the name of a domain controller and select Move. You can then select the site to which you want to move the domain-controller object.

Figure 1.5 shows the screen you'll see when you attempt to move a server. After the server is moved, all replication topology settings will be updated automatically. If you want to choose custom replication settings, you'll need to manually create connection objects.

FIGURE 1.5: Choosing a new site for a specific server

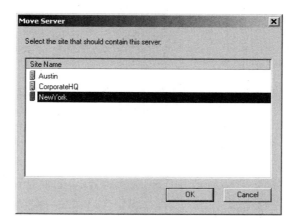

Creating Bridgehead Servers

By default, all servers in one site will communicate with the servers in another site. You can, however, further control replication between sites by using *bridgehead servers*. A bridgehead server specifies which domain controllers are preferred for transferring replication information between sites. Bridgehead servers minimize replication traffic in larger network environments and allow you to dedicate machines better equipped to receive replicated data.

Different bridgehead servers can be selected for IP and SMTP replication, thus allowing you to balance load. To create a bridgehead server for a site, right-click a domain controller and select Properties.

Necessary Procedures

This section contains exercises designed to increase your familiarity with Windows 2000 Active Directory. Without an understanding of the basic concepts and structure of Active Directory, more advanced topics will prove exceedingly difficult.

Promoting a Domain Controller

In this procedure you will install the first domain controller in the Active Directory environment. In order to complete these steps, you must have already installed and configured a Windows 2000 Server computer.

1. To start the Active Directory Installation Wizard, open the Configure Your Server applet in the Administrative Tools Program Group. Click the Active Directory option. At the bottom of the page, click the Start the Active Directory Wizard hyperlink. Alternatively, you can click on Start ➢ Run and type **dcpromo**.

2. Click Next on the first page of the Wizard to begin.

3. The first option to specify is the type of domain controller the server will be. To choose the Domain Controller Type, select Domain Controller for a New Domain and click Next. Note the warning that proceeding will delete all local accounts on the machine.

4. You will need to specify whether you want to create a new domain tree or make the new domain part of an existing tree. Because this will be the first domain in the Active Directory environment, choose Create a New Domain Tree and click Next.

5. Choose whether the new domain tree will be part of an existing forest or a new one you will create. Because this will be the first tree in the forest, select Create a New Forest of Domain Trees and click Next.

6. Specify a name for the new domain by typing in the full name of the DNS domain. For example, you can type **test.mycompany.com**. If you are not working in a test environment, be sure you have chosen a root domain name consistent for your organization that doesn't overlap with others. Click Next.

7. In order to preserve backward compatibility with earlier versions of Windows, you must provide a NetBIOS computer name. A NetBIOS name can be up to 15 characters. Although special characters are supported, you should limit yourself to the English alphabet characters and numbers. Type in the NetBIOS name for this machine and click Next.

8. In the Database and Log locations dialog box, you should specify the file system locations for the Active Directory database and log file. Microsoft recommends that these files reside on separate physical devices in order to improve performance and to provide for recoverability. The default file system location is in a directory called NTDS located within the system root. However, you can choose any folder located on a FAT, FAT32, or NTFS partition. Click Next.

9. Select a Shared System Volume location. The system volume folder will be used to store domain information that will be replicated to all other domain controllers in the domain. This folder must be stored on an NTFS 5 partition. The default location is in a directory called SYSVOL within the system root, but you can change this path based on your server configuration. Click Next.

10. As part of the promotion process, Windows 2000 will need you to set permissions on user and group objects. You can select permissions compatible with previous versions of Windows. This is a good choice if you're running in a mixed environment. If you are sure you will not be supporting non-Windows 2000 machines, however, you should choose Permissions Compatible Only with Windows 2000 Servers. It will implement stronger security settings. Once you have made the appropriate selection, click Next.

11. Provide a Directory Services Restore Mode Administrator password that can be used to restore the Active Directory in the event of the loss or corruption of the Active Directory. Note that this password is not required to correspond with passwords set for any other Windows 2000 account. Type the password, confirm it, and then click Next.

12. Based on the installation options you've selected, the Active Directory Installation Wizard will present a summary of your choices. It is a good idea to copy and paste this information into a text file for later reference. Verify the options and then click Next to begin the Active Directory installation process. When the necessary operations are complete, the Wizard will prompt you to click Finish.

Verifying Active Directory Installation with Event Viewer

In order to verify Active Directory installation with Event Viewer, the local machine must be configured as a domain controller.

1. Open the Event Viewer snap-in from the Administrative Tools program group.

2. In the left pane, select Directory Service.

3. In the right pane, notice that you can sort information by clicking column headings. For example, you can click on the Source column to sort by the service or process that reported the event.

4. Double-click an event in the list to see the details for that item. Note that you can click the Copy button to copy the event information to the clipboard. You can then paste the data into a document for later reference. Also, you can move between items using the up and down arrows. Click OK when you are done viewing an event.

5. You can filter specific events by right-clicking the Directory Service item in the left pane and selecting the Filter tab. Note that filtering does not remove entries from the event logs—it only restricts their display.

6. To verify the Active Directory installation, look for an event with information similar to the following:

   Event Type: Information

   Event Source: NTDS General

   Event Category: Service Control

   Event ID: 1000

   Date: 12/31/1999

   Time: 1:56:53 PM

   User: Everyone

Computer: DC1

Description: Microsoft Directory start-up complete, version 5.00.2160.1

7. When you're done viewing information in the Event Viewer, close the application.

Joining a Computer to an Active Directory Domain

In order to join a computer to a domain, you must have already installed and properly configured at least one Active Directory domain controller in your environment. In addition to the domain controller, you will need at least one other Windows 2000 computer. This computer may be an installation of Windows 2000 Professional or an installation of Windows 2000 Server not configured as a domain controller.

1. On the desktop of the computer to be joined to the new domain, right-click the My Computer icon and click Properties. Alternatively, you can right-click My Network Places, and choose Properties. From the Advanced menu, choose Advanced Settings.

2. Select the Network Identification tab. You will see the current name of the local computer as well as information on the workgroup or domain to which it belongs.

3. Click Properties to change the settings for this computer.

4. If you want to change the name of the computer, you can make the change here. This is useful if your domain has a specific naming convention for client computers. Otherwise, continue to the next step.

5. In the Member Of section, choose the Domain option. Type the name of the Active Directory domain that this computer should join. Click OK.

6. When prompted for the username and password of an account that has permissions to join computers to the domain, enter the information for an Administrator of the domain. Click OK to

commit the changes. If joining the domain was successful, you will see a dialog box welcoming you to the new domain.

7. You will be notified that you must reboot the computer before the changes take place. Select Yes when prompted to reboot.

Creating an OU Structure

This procedure is for creating an OU structure for a large organization. You must have first installed and configured at least one domain and have permissions to administer it.

1. Open the Active Directory Users and Computers administrative tool.

2. Right-click the name of the local domain and choose New ➤ Organizational Unit. You will see the dialog box shown in the following graphic. Notice that the box shows you the current context within which the OU will be created. Right now, you're creating a top-level OU, so the full path is simply the name of the domain.

3. Type in the name of the first OU. Click OU to create this object. Then create additional top-level OUs by right-clicking the name of the domain and choosing New ➤ Organizational Unit. Note that the order in which OUs are created is not important. In this exercise, we are simply using a method that emphasizes the hierarchical relationship.

4. Now, create second-level OUs within primary OUs by right-clicking the top-level OU and selecting New ➤ Organizational Unit. Type in the OU names.

5. Finally, it's time to create third-level OUs. Right-click a second-level OU and select New ➤ Organizational Unit. Type in the third-level names.

6. When you have completed the creation of the OUs, you should have a structure that looks similar to the one in Figure 1.6.

FIGURE 1.6: An OU structure

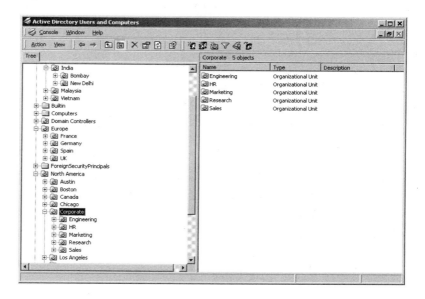

Modifying OU Structure

In order to modify the OU structure, you must have already created the structure in the last procedure, "Creating an OU Structure."

1. Open the Active Directory Users and Computers administrative tool.

2. To delete an OU, right-click the OU and click Delete. When prompted for confirmation, click Yes. Note that if this OU contained objects, all of the objects within the OU would have been automatically deleted as well.

3. To rename an OU, right-click the OU and select Rename. Type the new name and press Enter.

4. To move an OU, right-click the OU and select Move. In the Move dialog box, expand an OU and click the destination OU. Click OK to move the OU.

Using the Delegation of Control Wizard

In this procedure you will use the Delegation of Control Wizard to assign permissions to specific users within an Active Directory. In order to successfully complete these steps, you must first have created the objects in the previous procedures.

1. Open the Active Directory Users and Computers administrative tool.

2. Right-click an OU and select Delegate Control. The Delegation of Control Wizard will start. Click Next to begin making security settings.

3. In the Select Users, Computers, or Groups dialog box, select a user or group account and click Add. Click OK to accept this item, then click Next to continue.

4. In the Tasks to Delegate window, select Delegate the Following Common Tasks and place a check mark next to desired items:

   Create, delete, and manage user accounts

   Reset passwords on user accounts

   Read all user information

   Create, delete, and manage groups

   Modify the membership of a group

   Click Next to continue.

5. The Completion of the Delegation of Control Wizard dialog will provide a summary of the operations you have selected. To implement the changes, click Finish.

Assigning Single Master Operations

In this procedure you will assign Single Master Operations roles to various domain controllers within the environment. In order to complete these steps, you will require only one Active Directory domain controller.

1. Open the Active Directory Domains and Trusts administrative tool.

2. Right-click Active Directory Domains and Trusts, and choose Operations Master.

3. In the Change Operations Master dialog box, note that you can change the Operations Master by clicking the Change button. If you want to move this assignment to another computer, you will first need to connect to that computer and then make the change. Click Cancel to continue without making any changes. Close the Active Directory Domains and Trusts administrative tool.

4. Open the Active Directory Users and Computers administrative tool.

5. Right-click the name of a domain and select Operations Master. This will bring up the RID tab of the Operations Master dialog box. Notice that you can change the computer assigned to the role. In order to do so, you will first need to connect to the appropriate domain controller. Notice also there are similar tabs for the PDC and Infrastructure roles. Click Cancel to continue without making any changes.

6. Click Cancel to exit the Operations Master roles without making any changes.

7. When finished, close the Active Directory Users and Computers tool.

Global Catalog Servers

This procedure sets up Global Catalog Servers for a domain. It requires you have at least one operational domain controller.

1. Open the Active Directory Sites and Services administrative tool.

2. Find the name of the local domain controller within the list of objects and expand this object. Right-click NTDS Settings, and select Properties.

3. In the NTDS Settings Properties dialog box, type **Primary GC Server for Domain** in the Description field. Note that there is a check box that determines whether or not this computer contains a copy of the Global Catalog. If the box is checked, then this domain controller contains a subset of information from all other domains within the Active Directory environment. Select or deselect the Global Catalog check box, and then click OK to continue.

4. When finished, close the Active Directory Sites and Services administrative tool.

Creating Sites

In this procedure you will create new Active Directory sites. In order to complete this procedure, the local machine must be a domain controller. This procedure assumes you have not yet changed the default domain site configuration.

1. Open the Active Directory Sites and Services tool from the Administrative Tools program group.

2. Expand the Sites folder.

3. Right-click the Default-First-Site-Name item and choose Rename. Type the new name.

4. To create a new site, right-click the Sites object and select New Site.

5. Type the name of the site. Click the DEFAULTIPSITELINK item, and then click OK to create the site.

6. You will see a dialog box stating the actions you should take to finish the configuration of this site. Click OK to continue.

7. When finished, close the Active Directory Sites and Services tool.

Creating Subnets

Now you will create subnets and then assign them to sites. In order to complete the steps in this procedure, you must have first completed the previous one, "Creating Sites."

1. Open the Active Directory Sites and Services tool from the Administrative Tools program group.

2. Expand the Sites folder. Right-click the Subnets folder, and select New Subnet.

3. You will be prompted for information regarding the TCP/IP information for the new subnet. Type the address and mask values. You will see that the Name value has been automatically calculated. Click the site and then click OK to create the subnet.

4. Right-click the newly created subnet object and select Properties. On the Subnet tab, type in a subnet description. Click OK to continue.

5. When finished, close the Active Directory Sites and Services tool.

Creating Site Links and Site-Link Bridges

This procedure has you create links between sites. In order to complete the steps in this procedure, you must have created more than one site and subnet.

1. Open the Active Directory Sites and Services tool from the Administrative Tools program group.

2. Expand Sites ➤ Inter-Site Transports ➤ IP object. Right-click the DEFAULTIPSITELINK item in the right pane and select Rename. Give it a new name.

3. Right-click on your newly named link, and select Properties. Type in the description of the link. You should type in the Cost value and specify how often replication should occur. To create the site link, click OK.

4. Right-click the IP folder, and select New Site Link. Enter the name of the link. Add the sites to the site link and then click OK.

5. Right-click the CorporateDialup link, and select Properties. Type in the description, cost value, and replication frequency.

6. To specify that replication should occur only during certain times of the day, click the Change Schedule button. You can highlight the area between certain hours on certain days and click the Replication Not Available option. This will minimize replication traffic during peak hours. Click OK to accept the new schedule, and then OK again to create the site link.

7. Right-click the IP object, and select New Site Link Bridge. Type the name of the site-link bridge. Notice that the CorporateDialup and CorporateWAN site links are already added to the site-link bridge. Because there must be at least two site links in each bridge, you will not able to remove these links. Click OK to create the site link bridge.

8. When finished, close the Active Directory Sites and Services tool.

Creating Connection Objects

In this procedure you will create and configure a custom connection object to control Active Directory replication.

1. Open the Active Directory Sites and Services tool.

2. Find the Site that contains the local domain controller and expand this object.

3. Expand the name of the local domain controller. Right-click NTDS Settings and select New ≻ Connections. The Find Domain Controllers box will appear, showing a list of the servers available.

4. Highlight the name of the local server and click OK.

5. Type the name of the connection object. Click OK.

6. In the right pane of the window, right-click the Connection item, and select Properties.

7. Type the description. For the Transport, choose IP.

8. To modify the allowed times for replication, click the Change Schedule button. Highlight the hours and then click the frequency. This will reduce the frequency of replication during peak hours. Click OK to save the schedule.

9. When finished, click OK to save the properties of the connection object.

10. Close the Active Directory Sites and Services tool.

Moving Server Objects between Sites

In this procedure you will move a server object between sites. In order to complete these steps, you must have first completed the previous procedures.

1. Open the Active Directory Sites and Services Administrative tool.

2. Right-click the server to be moved and select Move.

3. Select the destination site. Clicking OK will move the server to that site.

4. To move the server back, right-click the moved site and then click Move. Select the site's original home.

5. When finished, close the Active Directory Sites and Services Administrative tool.

Exam Essentials

Understand what organizational units (OUs) are and how they are used.   OUs are logical divisions within a company's network structure. They're used to make the logical network more closely resemble the physical structure of the company.

Know how to install Active Directory and verify that it is working. Active Directory is installed through the use the Active Directory Installation Wizard, or DCPROMO. Once installed, it can be verified a variety of ways. These include using Event Viewer, using the Active Directory Administration Tools, and testing by connecting from a client.

Understand sites, subnets, site links, and site-link bridges.   A site is a logical grouping of computers, usually related to a close physical proximity. Sites are usually made up of one or more subnets. Site links and site-link bridges are used between sites to facilitate Directory Services replication. Also know how to install and configure each component.

Know the different operations master roles and what each one does.   The roles are Schema Master, Domain Naming Master, Relative ID (RID) Master, PDC Emulator Master, and Infrastructure Master. Review the section if you do not understand their roles within a domain.

Key Terms and Concepts

Active Directory   Microsoft's Active Directory technology is designed to store information about all objects within your network environment, including hardware, software, network devices, and users.

Active Directory Installation Wizard (DCPROMO)   The Wizard that allows you to promote a computer to a Domain Controller.

Active Directory replication   Process of synchronizing the Directory information on all Domain Controllers.

bridgehead servers   Servers that are a point through which all replication for that site flows.

delegation   One security authority giving responsibilities to a lower authority.

Delegation of Control Wizard   Utility that allows for the assignment of permissions to users or groups.

domain controllers   Computers that control security for a domain and are responsible for validating user logon requests.

Domain Naming Master   Computer responsible for keeping track of all domains within a forest.

File Allocation Table (FAT) file system   Widely used file system supported by DOS, Windows, and others.

forests   Logical groupings of computers that do not share a contiguous DNS namespace.

Global Catalog (GC) server   A repository of information about a subset of all objects within *all* Active Directory domains within a forest.

Group Policy   Collections of permissions that can be applied to objects within the Active Directory.

Infrastructure Master   A computer whose role is to ensure group-membership information stays synchronized within an Active Directory domain.

inheritance   The process of receiving security information from a parent directory or object.

mixed-mode Active Directory   Used when Windows NT servers are within the Active Directory structure.

native-mode Active Directory   Only Windows 2000 Domain Controllers are present.

organizational units (OUs)   Logical divisions within a company or organization. Used for security and grouping purposes.

Primary Domain Controller (PDC) Emulator   Machine responsible for maintaining backward compatibility with Windows NT domain controllers.

promotion   The process of making a member server into a domain controller.

Relative ID (RID) Master   Windows 2000 machine responsible for creating unique identifier values for objects within a domain whenever new Active Directory objects are created.

Schema Master   Machine responsible for propagating all changes to the schema (such as adding custom user attributes) to all other domain controllers within the forest.

security principals   An object for which individual security may be applied.

single-master operations   Actions for which there must be only one domain controller responsible. An example is a schema master or domain-naming master.

site A logical object that can contain servers and other objects related to Active Directory replication. Specifically, a site is a grouping of related subnets.

site links Logical connections that define a path between two Active Directory sites.

site-link bridges Used to connect site links together so that the relationship between two sites can be transitive.

subnet Group of computers in the same network determined by IP address and subnet mask.

trees Logical groupings of computers that share a common DNS namespace.

Windows NT File System (NTFS) File storage system supported only by Windows NT and Windows 2000.

Sample Questions

1. What should your primary concern be when developing a site structure for your network?

A. The number of departments within the company.

B. The physical location of resources within the company.

C. The number of OUs you plan on implementing.

D. The number of domain controllers within your company.

Answer: B. To reduce network-replication traffic, physical location should be the primary determining factor when planning sites.

2. You want to add a field to the information included on a user account showing the name of their pet. On which of the following servers can the change be made?

A. Any domain controller

B. Any member server

C. The Schema Master

D. None of the above

Answer: C. The Schema Master is the only server within the Active Directory on which changes to the schema can be made.

3. Which of the following operations does the Active Directory Installation Wizard not support?

A. Moving servers between domains

B. Demoting a domain controller to a server

C. Promoting a server to a domain controller

D. None of the above

Answer: A. The only way to move a domain controller between domains it to demote it from its current domain and then promote it into another domain.

Back up and restore Active Directory.

If you have deployed the Active Directory in your network environment, there's a good chance your users depend on it to do their jobs properly. From network authentications to files access to print and Web services, the Active Directory can be a mission-critical component of your business. Therefore, you should back up the Active Directory data regularly.

Critical Information

There are several reasons you'd want to back up data, including:

To protect against hardware failures   Computer hardware devices have finite lifetimes, and all hardware will eventually fail. Some types of failures, such as corrupted hard-disk drives, can result in significant data loss.

To protect against accidental deletion or modification of data
Although the threat of hardware failures is very real, in most environments, mistakes in modifying or deleting data are much more common. For example, suppose a systems administrator accidentally deletes all of the objects within a specific OU. Clearly, it's very important to be able to retrieve this information from a backup.

To keep historical information   Users and systems administrators sometimes modify files and then later find they require access to an older version of a file. Or a file is accidentally deleted, but a user does not discover that fact until much later. By keeping backups over time, you can recover information from these prior backups when necessary.

To protect against malicious deletion or modification of data
Even in the most secure environments, it is conceivable that unauthorized users (or authorized ones with malicious intent!) could delete or modify information. In such cases, the loss of data might require valid backups from which to restore critical information.

Windows 2000 includes a Backup utility, shown in Figure 1.7, designed to back up operating-system files and the Active Directory data store. It allows for basic backup functionality, such as scheduling backup jobs and selecting which files to back up.

FIGURE 1.7: The Backup utility in Windows 2000

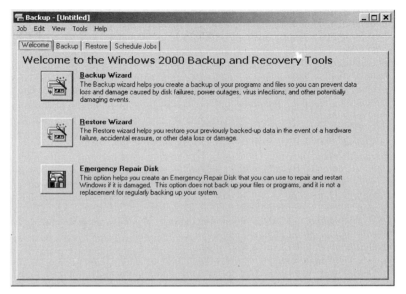

Backup Types

Although it is possible to back up all of the files in the file system during each backup operation, it's sometimes more convenient to back up only selected files (such as those that have changed since the last backup operation). To this end there are several types of backups you can perform.

How do you know which files have changed since the last backup? More importantly, how does Windows Backup know? The "backed-up" status of a file is tracked by using an Archive bit. If changes have been made to a file since its last backup, the bit is set to 1, or Active. (In Windows, you see a check in the Archive box of the file's Properties.) In most backups once the file is backed up, the bit is set back to 0. You can view the attributes of a file by right-clicking it and selecting Properties. Click Advanced, and you will see the option File Is Ready for Archiving.

Normal

A *normal backup* backs up all of the selected files and then marks them as backed up. This option is usually used when a full system backup is made.

Copy

A *copy backup* backs up all selected files, but does not mark them as backed up. This is useful when you want to make additional backups of files for moving files off-site or making multiple copies of the same data or for archival purposes. Copies are usually made of the whole system.

Incremental

An *incremental backup* copies any selected files that are marked as ready for backup and then marks the files as backed up. When the next incremental backup is run, only the files that are not marked as having been backed up are stored. Incremental backups are used in conjunction with full (normal) backups. The general process is to make a full backup and then to make subsequent incremental backups. The benefit to this method is reduced backup times and disk or tape storage requirements.

When recovering information from this type of backup method, you will be required to first restore the full backup and then to restore each of the incremental backups.

Differential

A *differential backup* is similar in purpose to an incremental backup with one important exception: a differential backup copies all files that are marked for backup but does not mark the files as backed up. When restoring files in a situation that uses normal and differential backups, you only need to restore the normal backup and the latest differential backup.

Whereas copy backups back up the files you select (requiring manual intervention), differential backups automatically back up only the files that have changed since their last marked backup.

Daily

A daily backup backs up all files that have changed during the current day. This operation uses the file time/date stamps to determine which files should be backed up and does not mark the files as having been backed up.

NOTE   Systems administrators might choose to combine normal, daily, incremental, and differential backup types as part of the same backup plan. In general, however, it is sufficient to use only one or two methods (for example, normal backups with incremental backups). If you require a combination of multiple backup types, be sure that you fully understand which types of files are being backed up.

Emergency Repair

Another option is to create an Emergency Repair Disk (ERD). In the event that boot or configuration information is lost, the ERD and Windows 2000 Repair process can restore a system.

WARNING   The Emergency Repair Disk does not serve as a substitute for system backups. It only backs up portions of the registry and critical system files needed during the boot process.

Backing Up System State Information

When planning to back up and restore the Active Directory, the most important component is the *System State*. System State information includes the components that the Windows 2000 operating system relies on for normal operations. The Windows 2000 Backup utility allows you to back up the System State to another type of media (such as a hard disk, network share, or tape device). Specifically, it will back up the following components for a Windows 2000 domain controller:

Active Directory   The Active Directory data store is the heart of the Active Directory. It contains all the information necessary to create and manage such network resources as users and computers.

In most environments that use the Active Directory, users and systems administrators rely on the proper functioning of these services to do their jobs.

Boot files   These are the files required for booting the Windows 2000 operating system and can be used in the case of boot-file corruption.

COM+ Class Registrations Database   Applications that run on a Windows 2000 computer might require the registration of share-code components. As part of the System State backup process, Windows 2000 will store all of the information related to Component Object Model+ (COM+) components so this information can be quickly and easily restored.

Registry   The Windows 2000 Registry is a central repository of information related to the operating-system configuration (such as desktop and network settings), user settings, and application settings. Therefore, the Registry is absolutely vital to the proper functioning of Windows 2000.

SysVol   The SysVol directory includes data and files shared between the domain controllers within an Active Directory domain. Many operating-system services rely on this information for proper functioning.

When you back up the System State information, the Windows 2000 Backup utility automatically backs up all of these types of files.

Scheduling Backups

In addition to specifying which files to back up, you can schedule backup jobs to occur at specific times. Planning *when* to perform backups is just as important as deciding what to backup. Performing backup operations can reduce overall system performance; therefore, you should plan to back up during times of minimal activity on your servers.

Restoring the Active Directory

Once your backups are made, you have a measure of fault recovery for your network. If Active Directory becomes corrupt or a domain controller crashes, you have your backups to get the network running again.

The Active Directory has been designed with fault tolerance in mind. For example, it is highly recommended that each domain have at least two domain controllers. Each of these domain controllers contains a copy of the Active Directory data store. Should one of the domain controllers fail, the other one can take over. When the failed server is repaired, it can then be promoted to a domain controller in the existing environment. Thus, the failed domain controller is restored without incurring any downtime for end users.

Performing an Authoritative Restore of Active Directory

Windows 2000 and the Active Directory allow you to perform an *authoritative restore*. An authoritative restore specifies a domain controller as having the authoritative (or master) copy of the Active Directory data store. When other domain controllers communicate with the authoritative domain controller, their information will be overwritten with that stored on the authoritative machine.

When restoring Active Directory information on a Windows 2000 domain controller, the Active Directory services must not be running, because the restore of System State information requires full access to system files and the Active Directory data store. If you attempt to restore System State information while the domain controller is active, you will see an error message: The system state cannot be restored while the Active Directory service is running.

In general, restoring data and operating-system files is a straightforward process. It is important to note that restoring a System State backup will replace the existing Registry, SysVol, and Active Directory files. This process uses the Ntdsutil utility to set the authoritative restore mode for a domain controller after the System State is restored, but before the domain controller is rebooted.

 In addition to restoring the entire Active Directory database, you can also restore just specific subtrees within the Active Directory using the Restore Subtree command. Restore Subtree is useful in the case of an accidental deletion of isolated material.

Following the authoritative-restore process, the Active Directory should be updated to the time of the last backup. Furthermore, all other domain controllers for this domain will have their Active Directory information overwritten by the results of the restore operation. The end result is an Active Directory environment that has been recovered from media.

Necessary Procedures

There are two procedures you need to know how to perform for this objective: how to back up the Active Directory and how to restore the Active Directory.

Backing up the Active Directory

Backing up the Active Directory is performed through the Windows 2000 Backup utility. Make sure to plan a backup schedule that meets the needs of your organization.

1. Open the Backup utility by clicking Start ➤ Programs ➤ Accessories ➤ System Tools ➤ Backup.

2. To start the backup process using the Backup Wizard, click the Backup Wizard button.

3. Click Next to start the backup process.

4. In the What to Backup dialog box, select Only Back Up the System State Data. Note that there are also options to back up all files on the computer and to back up only specific information. Click Next to continue.

5. Next you'll need to select where you want to back up this information. If you have a tape drive installed on the local computer, you'll have the option to back up to tape. Otherwise, the option will be disabled, and you can only select File. Select File for the backup media type, and then enter the full path and filename for the backup file. The default file extension for a Windows 2000 Backup file is .BKF. You should be sure the selected folder has sufficient space to store the System State information (which is usually more than 300MB). Click Next to continue.

6. The Windows 2000 Backup Wizard will now display a summary of the options you selected for backup. Verify that the files to be backed up and the location information are correct. Note that by clicking the Advanced button, you can select from among different backup types (such as copy, differential, and incremental) and can choose whether remote-storage files will be backed up. Click Finish to begin the backup process.

7. The backup process will begin, and the approximate size of the backup will be calculated. On most systems, the backup operation will take at least several minutes. The exact amount of time required will be based on server load, server hardware configuration, and the size of the System State information.

8. When the backup operation has completed, you can click the Report button to see information about the backup process (including any errors that might have occurred). Optionally, you can save this report as a text file to examine later.

9. When finished, click Close and then close the Backup application.

Restoring the System State and the Active Directory

In order to completely restore the System State and the Active Directory, you must have first completed the steps to back up the Active Directory.

1. Reboot the local machine. During system start-up, press the F8 key to enter the Windows 2000 Server boot options.

2. From the boot menu, choose Directory Services Restore Mode (Windows 2000 Domain Controllers Only) and press Enter. The operating system will begin to boot in safe mode.

3. Log on to the computer as a member of the *local* Administrators group. Note that you cannot log on using any Active Directory accounts since network services and the Active Directory have not been started.

4. You will see a message warning you the machine is running in safe mode and certain services will not be available. For example, a minimal set of drivers will have been loaded, and you will not have access to the network. Click OK to continue.

5. When the operating system has finished booting, open the Backup utility by clicking Start ➢ Programs ➢ Accessories ➢ System Tools ➢ Backup.

6. On the main screen of the Backup utility, click the Restore Wizard icon.

7. Click Next to begin the Restore Wizard.

8. Expand the File item by clicking the plus sign. Expand the Media item and then click the plus sign next to the System State icon.

9. Enter the path and file name of the backup file that you created during the previous procedure. The Backup utility will scan the file for the appropriate backup information.

10. Place a check mark next to the System State item, and then click Next.

11. The Restore Wizard will display a summary of the recovery options you selected.

12. Click the Advanced button to specify the location for the restored files. The options include the original location, an alternate location, or a single folder. Verify that the original location option is selected and then click Next.

13. You will then be prompted to specify how you want files to be restored. Select the Always Replace the File on the Disk option and click next.

14. For the Advanced Restore Options dialog box, use the default settings (none of the boxes checked). Click Next.

15. To begin the Restore operation, click Finish. Windows 2000 Backup will begin to restore the System State files to the local computer.

16. Once the System State information has been restored, you will see statistics related to the recovery operation. To view detailed information, click the Report button. When you are finished, click Close.

17. You will be prompted about whether you want to restart the computer. Select No. Close the Windows 2000 Backup application.

18. Now you will need to place the domain controller in authoritative-restore mode. To do this, click Start ➢ Run and type **cmd**. At the command prompt, type **ntdsutil** and press Enter. Note that you can type a question mark and press Enter to view help information for the various commands available with the Ntdsutil application.

19. At the Ntdsutil prompt, type **authoritative restore** and press Enter.

20. At the authoritative-restore prompt, type **restore database** and press Enter. You will be asked whether you want to perform an authoritative restore. Click Yes.

21. The Ntdsutil application will begin the authoritative-restore process. When the process has completed, type **quit** twice to exit the Ntdsutil. Then close the command prompt by typing **exit**.

22. Finally, click Start ➢ Shut Down and restart the computer. Following a reboot of the operating system, the Active Directory and System State information will be current to the point of the last backup.

Exam Essentials

Understand the different types of backups Windows 2000 can perform. Review the differences between normal, copy, incremental, differential, and daily backups.

Know what backing up the System State backs up. The System State includes the Active Directory, boot files, COM+ Class Registrations Database, the Registry, and SysVol.

Understand what an authoritative restore is. The authoritative restore process specifies a domain controller as having the authoritative (or master) copy of the Active Directory data store. When other domain controllers communicate with this domain controller, their information will be overwritten with the information stored on the authoritative machine. This becomes important when you have multiple domain controllers. It lets the administrator specify which domain controller is the master.

Know the key points for restoring the Active Directory. First, use Directory Services Restore Mode to start the restore process. Once in restore mode, Windows 2000 Backup lets you start the Restore Wizard. Ntdsutil lets you perform an authoritative restore.

Key Terms and Concepts

archive bit   File property that shows whether the file has changed since it was backed up last.

authoritative restore   The authoritative-restore process specifies a domain controller as having the authoritative (or master) copy of the Active Directory data store.

boot files   Files necessary for the boot up of a Windows 2000 computer.

copy backup   Backs up selected files on the system, but does *not* mark them as being backed up.

daily backup   Backs up only the files modified during that day. Uses date and time stamps.

differential backup   Only backs up files that have changed since the last backup. Does not mark the files as having been backed up.

Emergency Repair Disk   Disk that contains backups of portions of the Registry and critical boot files.

incremental backup   Only backs up files that have changed since the last backup. Marks the files as having been backed up.

normal backup   Backs up all files on the system, and marks them as being backed up.

Registry   Database that stores all critical Windows 2000 configuration information.

System State   System State information includes the components that the Windows 2000 operating system relies on for normal operations. These include the Active Directory, boot files, COM+ Class Registrations Database, the Registry, and SysVol.

SysVol   The directory that includes data and files shared between the domain controllers within an Active Directory domain.

Sample Questions

1. Following an authoritative restore of the entire Active Directory database, what will happen to the copy of the Active Directory on other domain controllers for the same domain?

   A. The other domain controllers will be automatically demoted.

   B. The copies of the Active Directory on other domain controllers will be overwritten.

   C. The information on all domain controllers will be merged.

   D. Nothing.

   Answer: B. In an authoritative restore of the entire Active Directory database, the restored copy will override information stored on other domain controllers.

2. Which of the following are backed up as part of the Windows 2000 System State on a domain controller?

   A. Registry

   B. COM+ Registration information

   C. Boot files

   D. Active Directory database information

   E. All of the above

   Answer: E. Backing up the System State backs up all of the above.

3. What type of backup will back up only the files that have changed since the last backup, but not mark them as being backed up?

   A. Full

   B. Daily

   C. Incremental

   D. Differential

   Answer: D. A differential back up is the only one that backs up the files but does not mark them as being backed up.

Chapter

2

Installing, Configuring, Managing, Monitoring, and Troubleshooting DNS for Active Directory

---

MICROSOFT EXAM OBJECTIVES COVERED IN THIS CHAPTER:

▶ **Install, configure, and troubleshoot DNS for Active Directory.** *(pages 64 – 95)*

- Integrate Active Directory DNS zones with non–Active Directory DNS zones.

- Configure zones for dynamic updates.

▶ **Manage, monitor, and troubleshoot DNS.** *(pages 95 – 104)*

- Manage replication of DNS data.

When Microsoft introduced Windows 2000, a major philosophical shift took place. Before Windows 2000, Microsoft computers used a simple naming convention called NetBIOS names to identify unique machines on the network. Whereas the convention worked for smaller networks, the problem of duplicate names on large networks emerged.

The computer industry, Microsoft included, is headed toward the "global network," where all resources will conceivably be available on all workstations. To this end, the X.500 naming convention was introduced, and Microsoft decided to follow it. X.500 provides for unique naming of all objects on a network, regardless of network size. In order to help resolve the names, called host names or Fully Qualified Domain Names, over TCP/IP, DNS servers are required.

The installation, configuration, and management of DNS are critical to the operation of a Windows 2000 network. Understanding how DNS works will also make the exam much easier.

Install, configure, and troubleshoot DNS for Active Directory.

Understanding DNS is vital to the deployment of the Active Directory and is a prerequisite for installing and configuring domain controllers. A common mistake made by systems administrators is underestimating the importance and complexity of DNS. Fully understanding DNS is not an easy task, especially for those who have limited experience with TCP/IP. The Active Directory relies on DNS to find clients, servers, and network services throughout your environment. Clients also rely on DNS to find file, print, and other resources they require.

Critical Information

The *Domain Name System* (DNS) is a TCP/IP standard designed to resolve host names to IP addresses. Thanks largely to the tremendous rise in popularity of the Internet, most environments have transitioned to the *Transmission Control Protocol/Internet Protocol* (TCP/IP) as their primary networking protocol. Microsoft is no exception. All current versions of Microsoft operating systems support TCP/IP, as do almost all other modern operating systems. Since the introduction of Windows NT 4, TCP/IP has been the default protocol installed.

NOTE   The first part of this section reviews DNS structure, design, and theory. You need such background information to better understand the test objectives covered a little later.

TCP/IP is actually a collection of different technologies that allow computers to operate together on a single network. Some of the major advantages of the protocol include widespread support for hardware, software, and network devices, reliance on a system of standards, and scalability.

NOTE   For a detailed discussion of TCP/IP, please see *MCSE: Windows 2000 Directory Services Administration Study Guide* (Sybex, 2000).

DNS is a hierarchical naming system that contains a distributed database of name-to-IP address mappings. DNS names are much friendlier and easier to remember than IP addresses. For example, every time you enter a URL (such as www.microsoft.com), your computer makes a query to a DNS server that resolves the name to an IP address. From then on, all communications between your computer and that Web server take place using the IP address.

The Active Directory uses DNS to locate servers and clients. Microsoft has included a DNS-server service with the Windows 2000 operating system, along with many advanced features (some of which are not yet industry standard) that reduce the complexity of maintaining DNS databases.

The Anatomy of a DNS Name

DNS servers are designed to resolve network addresses with friendly names. DNS names take the form of a series of alphanumeric strings separated by decimal points. Together, the various portions of a DNS name form what is called the *DNS namespace,* and each address within it must be unique. All of the following examples are valid DNS names:

- `microsoft.com`

- `www.microsoft.com`

- `sales.microsoft.com`

- `engineering.microsoft.com`

The left-most portion of the name is called the *host name* and refers to the actual name of a machine. The remaining portions are part of the domain name and uniquely specify the network on which the host resides. The full name is referred to as the *Fully Qualified Domain Name* (FQDN). For example, the host name might be `engineering`, whereas the FQDN is `engineering.microsoft.com`.

There are several features and limitations to note about a DNS name:

The name is hierarchical.   The domains listed at the right-most side of the address are higher-level domains. As you move left, each portion zooms in on the actual host. In other words, as you read from left to right, you are moving from the specific host name to its various containers.

The name is case insensitive.   Although DNS names are sometimes printed in mixed case for clarity, the case of the characters has no relevance.

Each FQDN on a given network must be unique.   No two machines on the same network may have the same FQDN; each machine must be uniquely identified.

Only certain characters are allowed.   Each portion of the DNS name may include only standard English characters, decimal numbers, and dashes.

There are maximum lengths for addresses.   A DNS address can have a maximum length of 255 characters, and each name within the full name can have up to 63 characters.

The Root

In order to resolve friendly names with IP addresses, there must be some starting point. All Internet DNS names originate from one address, known as the root. This address typically does not have a name and is represented in the DNS as a period ("."). The InterNIC is responsible for managing the root servers. Registered in the root servers are the standard top-level domains with which most people are familiar.

Many organizations worldwide require domain names to be resolved starting at the root. That is the purpose of the top-level domains. On the Internet there are several established top-level domains. Table 2.1 provides a list of the common North American top-level domains. Each domain space is reserved for a particular type of user, also shown in the table.

TABLE 2.1:   North American Top-Level Domain Names

Top-Level Domain	Typical Users
.com	Commercial organizations
.edu	Educational institutions
.gov	U.S. governmental organizations
.int	International organizations
.mil	U.S. military organizations

T A B L E   2 . 1 :   North American Top-Level Domain Names *(continued)*

Top-Level Domain	Typical Users
.net	Large network providers (such as Internet Service Providers)
.org	Non-profit organizations

In addition to these top-level domain names, there are many country codes for top-level domains throughout the world. Each is managed by its own authority. For example, a DNS name that is based in the United Kingdom may have a domain name of mycompany.co.uk. If you require a foreign-domain-name registration, you should inquire with the country's name service provider.

In order for an organization's own domain name to be resolved on the Internet, it must request that a second-level domain name be added to the global top-level DNS servers. Several registrars can perform this function worldwide.

TIP   For more information on registering a domain name for your own organization, see www.internic.net. There, you will find a list of common registrars available worldwide. There is a nominal charge for each domain name you register.

The name registered on the Internet is known as a second-level domain name. Company1.com, for example, would be considered a second-level domain name. Within an organization, however, all of the domain names would be subdomains of this one. As an example, server1.sales.company1.com would refer to the server1 computer in the sales subdomain, registered to the company1.com domain.

A major consideration of DNS namespace configuration is whether you want to use public Internet Service Providers (ISPs) for name resolution. If not, you will host your own domain name. As such, you may choose any top-level domain name you like, but your servers cannot be made directly accessible on the Internet because public names must be guaranteed unique. For example, you might choose the names sales.mycompany and engineering.mycompany. Although these are perfectly valid DNS names for internal use, Internet users will not be able to access them.

You could use public Internet authorities and employ names such as sales.mycompany.com and engineering.mycompany.com. You would then need to rely on the DNS servers managed by your ISP (Internet Service Provider) for external name resolution.

Parent and Child Names

Once an organization has registered its own domain name, it must list that name on a DNS server, either within the organization or at a third-party location such as with an ISP. In either case, systems and network administrators can start adding names to their DNS servers using the top-level domain name.

For example, if you want to make three computers available on the Internet, you would first need to register a second-level domain name, such as mycompany.com. You could then choose to add your own domain names, such as the following:

- www.mycompany.com

- mail.mycompany.com

- computer1.northamerica.sales.mycompany.com

Each of these domain names must be listed on the DNS server as a *resource record* (RR). The records consist of a domain name mapped to an IP address. When users try to access one of these machines (through a Web browser, for example), the name will be resolved with the appropriate TCP/IP address.

DNS servers are responsible for carrying out various name-resolution functions. One such function fulfills DNS name-mapping requests. If a DNS server has information about the specific host name specified in the request, it simply returns the appropriate information to the client. If it does not, the DNS server can obtain that information from another DNS server through the process of *name resolution*. Simply put, through name resolution a DNS server queries other DNS servers to resolve names of which it has no knowledge. You can see how a worldwide network of names can be formed. Later in this chapter, you'll see the various steps required to facilitate worldwide DNS communication.

DNS Zones

A *DNS zone* is a portion of the DNS namespace over which a specific DNS server has authority. Zones exist for accurate name resolution on the Internet.

NOTE There is an important distinction between DNS zones and DNS domains. Although both use hierarchical names and require name resolution, DNS zones do not necessarily map directly to DNS domains. That is to say, one DNS domain may be made up of multiple DNS zones.

Every DNS server can be configured to be responsible for one or more DNS domains. The DNS server is then known as the authoritative source of address information for that zone. Generally, if you use only a single DNS domain, you will have only one zone. Remember, there can be a many-to-many relationship between domains (which are used to create a logical naming structure) and zones (which refer primarily to the physical structure of a DNS implementation).

When you add subdomains, you have two options. You can allow the original DNS server to continue functioning as the authority for the *parent and child domains*. Or you can choose to create another DNS zone and give a different server authority over it. The process of giving authority for specific domains to other DNS servers is known as delegation.

The main reasons for delegation are performance and administration. Multiple DNS servers in a large network can help distribute the load involved in resolving names. It can also help administer security by allowing only certain types of records to be modified by specified systems administrators.

DNS Server Roles

One potential problem with configuring specific DNS servers as authorities for their own domains is fault tolerance. What happens if an authoritative server becomes unavailable? Theoretically, none of the names for the resources in that zone would be resolved to network addresses—a potentially serious problem for networks of any size. For example, if the primary server for the `sales.mycompany.com` zone becomes unavailable (and there are no secondary servers in that zone), users will not be able to find resources such as `server1.sales.mycompany.com` or `workstation1.sales.mycompany.com`. In order to prevent the potential network problems of a single failed server, the DNS specification supports multiple servers per zone. To maintain a distributed and hierarchical naming system, DNS servers can assume several different roles at once.

Primary Server

Each DNS zone must have one *primary DNS server*. The primary server is responsible for maintaining all of the records for the DNS zone and contains the primary copy of the DNS database. Additionally, all updates of records occur on the primary server. You will want to create and add primary servers whenever you create a new DNS domain. When creating child domains, however, you may want to use the primary server from the parent domain.

Secondary Server

A *secondary DNS server* contains a database of the same information on the primary name server and can resolve DNS requests. The main purpose of a secondary server is fault tolerance. If the primary server becomes unavailable, name resolution would still occur. Therefore, it is a good general practice to have at least one secondary server in each zone.

Secondary DNS servers can also increase performance by offloading some of the traffic from the primary server. Further, secondary servers are often located within each location that has high-speed network access, to prevent DNS queries from having to run across slow WAN connections. For example, if the `mycompany.com` organization has two remote offices, you may want to place a secondary DNS server in each.

This way, when clients require name resolution, they will contact the nearest server for this IP address information, thus preventing unnecessary WAN traffic.

Although secondary servers are beneficial, too many of them can cause increases in network traffic due to replication. Therefore, always weigh the benefits and drawbacks.

Master Server

Master DNS servers handle replication of the DNS database between primary and secondary servers within a particular zone. Usually, the primary server also serves as the master server, but these tasks can be separated for performance reasons.

Caching-Only Server

Caching-only DNS servers are DNS servers that only assist clients in resolving DNS names to network addresses. Caching-only servers are not authoritative for any DNS zone, and they don't contain copies of the zone files. Caching-only servers just contain mappings as a result of resolved queries and will lose the RAM-cached mapping information when shut down. Therefore, they are installed only for performance reasons. A good environment may be a site with slow connectivity to off-site DNS servers.

Zone Transfers

DNS zone information must be consistent between the primary and secondary servers. The process used to keep the servers synchronized is known as a *zone transfer*. When a secondary DNS server is configured for a zone, it first performs a zone transfer, during which it obtains a copy of the primary server's address database.

Zone transfers can create a great deal of network traffic. (One of the major advantages to using caching-only servers is they do not perform zone transfers.) There are two types of zone transfers:

All-Zone Transfer (AXFR)   An *all-zone transfer* happens when a secondary server comes online. AXFR downloads all zone information to the secondary server.

Incremental Zone Transfer (IXFR)   An *incremental zone transfer* only transfers updates to the secondary server, reducing the amount of traffic created by the transfer process.

NOTE   Not all DNS servers support IXFRs. Windows NT 4's DNS services and earlier implementations of other DNS services require a full zone transfer of the entire database in order to update records. This can sometimes cause excessive network traffic.

DNS Resource Records

It's time to look at the information stored within the DNS database. Table 2.2 provides a list of the types of records and their functions. For example, if a client is attempting to send e-mail, the DNS server should respond with the IP address corresponding to the Mail Exchanger (MX) record of the domain.

TABLE 2.2:   DNS Resource Record Types

Resource Record Type	Meaning	Notes
A	Address	Used to map host names to IP addresses; multiple A records may be used to map to a single IP address
CNAME	Canonical Name	Used as an alias or a nickname for a host (in addition to the A record)
MX	Mail Exchange	Specifies the Simple Mail Transfer Protocol (SMTP) e-mail server address for the domain
NS	Name Server	Specifies the IP address of DNS servers for the domain

TABLE 2.2: DNS Resource Record Types *(continued)*

Resource Record Type	Meaning	Notes
PTR	Pointer	Used for reverse lookup operations
RP	Responsible Person	Specifies information about the individual responsible for maintaining DNS information
SOA	Start of Authority	Specifies the authoritative server for a zone
SRV	Service Resource Records	Specifies server services available on a host; used by the Active Directory to identify domain controllers; the standard for SRV records has not yet been finalized

Planning for Microsoft DNS

One of the major benefits of Microsoft DNS is the ability to manage and replicate the DNS database as a part of the Active Directory, which allows for automating much of the administration of the DNS service while still keeping information up-to-date.

With respect to your DNS environment, you'll want to plan for the use of various DNS servers, in the possible roles of primary, secondary, master, and caching-only servers. With respect to the Active Directory, DNS services are absolutely vital. Without the proper functioning of DNS, Active Directory clients and servers will not be able to locate each other, and network services will essentially not be provided.

Planning DNS Zones

The first step in planning for DNS server deployment is to determine the size and layout of your DNS zones. In the simplest configurations, there will be a single Active Directory domain and a single DNS zone. This configuration usually meets the needs of single-domain environments.

When multiple domains are considered, you generally need to make some choices. In some environments, you might choose to use only a single zone that spans all of the domains. In other cases, you might want to break zones apart for administrative and performance reasons.

The DNS zone configuration you choose is largely independent of the Active Directory configuration. That is, for any given Active Directory configuration, you could use any setup of zones, as long as all names can be properly resolved. With that said, make no mistake—the proper functioning of DNS zones is critical to the functionality of the Active Directory.

Planning Server Roles

For fault tolerance, be sure each DNS zone consists of one primary DNS server and at least one secondary server. If the primary DNS server fails, the secondary can still provide name resolution. However, you will need to restore or replace the primary DNS server in order to make updates to the DNS zone information.

Generally, you will want to make the primary DNS server the master server for the zone. For performance reasons, however, you can choose separate machines.

Caching-only servers are generally used when you want to make DNS information available for multiple computers that do not have a fast or reliable connection to the main network. Because they do not have any authority over specific zones, the decision to use caching-only servers is generally based on the physical network layout.

Installing and Configuring a DNS Server

Microsoft made DNS service installation extremely simple. But don't be lulled into a false sense of security; you must still be thorough in your understanding and planning for a DNS configuration. If not, you will not be able to troubleshoot problems when DNS malfunctions.

Adding DNS Zones

After installing DNS, you'll need to configure it for your specific environment. The most important aspect of configuring the DNS properly is planning. Make sure to include a standard primary forward-lookup zone.

Configuring DNS Zone Properties

Once you have properly configured zones for your DNS server, you can make additional configuration settings for each zone by right-clicking its name within the DNS administrative tool and selecting Properties. The following tabs and settings are available for forward-lookup zones:

General The general tab allows you set various options for the forward-lookup zone.

Using this tab (see Figure 2.1), you can pause the DNS service. When the service is paused, it continues to run, but clients cannot complete name-resolution requests from this machine.

A second option is to change the type of zone. Choices include primary, secondary, and Active Directory–integrated (available only if the Active Directory is installed).

You can specify the name of the DNS zone file. Allowing dynamic updates is extremely useful for reducing the management and administration headaches associated with creating resource records.

Finally, you can specify aging and scavenging properties for this zone.

FIGURE 2.1: Setting zone properties with the General tab

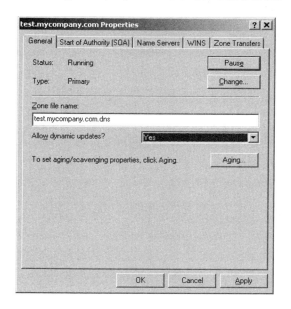

Start of Authority (SOA)   The SOA tab allows you to specify information regarding the authority of the DNS server (see Figure 2.2).

The Serial Number text box is used to determine whether a zone transfer is needed to keep any secondary servers up-to-date. For example, if a secondary server has a serial number of 7, and the SOA serial number is set to 6, the secondary server will request a zone transfer.

The Primary Server text box allows you to designate the primary DNS server for the zone.

The Responsible Person (RP) text box allows you to specify contact information for the systems administrator of the DNS server.

The Refresh Interval text box and drop-down menu are used to stipulate how often a secondary zone should verify its information. Lower times result in greater accuracy but can cause increased network traffic.

The Retry Interval text box and drop-down menu set how often zone transfers will be requested.

The Expires After text box and drop-down menu let you designate how long secondary DNS servers must try to request updated information before resource records expire.

The Minimum (default) TTL text box indicates how long a resource record will be considered current. If you are working in an environment where many changes are expected, a lower TTL value can help in maintaining the accuracy of information.

FIGURE 2.2: Setting zone properties with the SOA tab

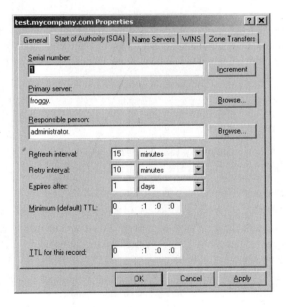

Name Servers   The Name Servers tab shows a list of DNS servers for the specified domain. You can add specific DNS servers based on the configuration of your network. Generally, the list of name servers will include the primary name server and any secondary name servers for that zone.

WINS   This tab allows you to set options for allowing Windows Internet Naming Service (WINS) lookups to resolve DNS names. WINS and DNS issues are covered later in this chapter.

Zone Transfers   Using the options on this tab, you can select which servers will be allowed to serve as a secondary server for the forward-lookup zones specified in the properties for the zone. The default option allows any server to request a zone transfer, but you can restrict this by specifying specific IP addresses or allowing only the name servers listed on the Name Servers tab to request transfers. Setting restrictions on zone transfers can increase security by preventing unauthorized users from copying the entire DNS database.

Configuring DNS Server Options

DNS record databases would tend to become disorganized and filled with outdated information if processes that periodically removed unused records were not present. The removal of inactive or outdated entries in the DNS database is known as *scavenging*. Systems administrators use scavenging to configure refreshing of DNS records based on a certain time setting. When the DNS record has not been refreshed for a certain amount of time, the next DNS query forces the record to be updated. By default, the DNS server is not configured to perform this process at all.

To implement scavenging in the DNS snap-in, you should right-click the name of the server or DNS zone for which you want the settings to apply and choose Set Aging/Scavenging. The aging and scavenging settings you specify will apply to all of the DNS zones managed by that server. As shown in Figure 2.3, you can specify two different options:

No-Refresh Interval   The interval allows you to specify the *minimum* amount of time that must elapse before a DNS record is refreshed. Higher values can reduce network traffic but may cause outdated information to be returned to clients.

Refresh Interval   The option allows you to specify the amount of time between when the no-refresh interval expires and when the resource record may be refreshed. Lower values can provide for greater accuracy in information but may increase network traffic.

FIGURE 2.3: Setting aging and scavenging options

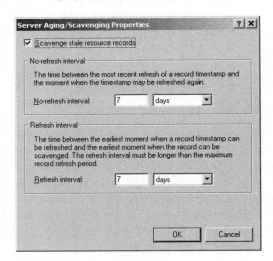

Several other DNS server options can be set to maximize performance in your network environment. To access the properties of the DNS server using the DNS snap-in, right-click the name of the server and choose Properties. The following options will be available:

Interfaces   On servers enabled with multiple network adapters, you might want to provide DNS services on only one of the interfaces. The default option is to allow DNS requests on all interfaces, but you can limit operations to specific adapters by clicking the Only the Following IP Addresses option (see Figure 2.4).

FIGURE 2.4: Selecting DNS server interfaces

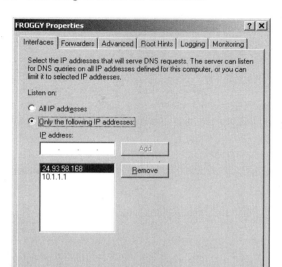

Forwarders   DNS forwarding can be configured to relay all DNS requests that cannot be resolved by this server to one or more specific machines. To configure forwarders, check the box and specify the IP address of one or more DNS servers. If you check the Do Not Use Recursion option, name resolution will occur only through the configured forwarders.

Advanced   The DNS service has several advanced options (see Figure 2.5). For example, you can disable DNS recursion for the entire server by checking the appropriate box. For more details, see the Windows 2000 Help files.

FIGURE 2.5: Advanced DNS server configuration options

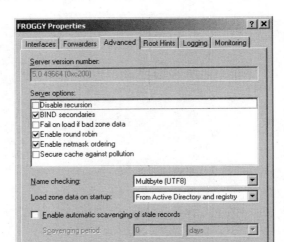

Root Hints In order to resolve domain names on the Internet, the local DNS server must know the identities of the worldwide root servers. By default, the Microsoft DNS server is configured with several valid root IP addresses (see Figure 2.6). Additionally, you can add or modify the root hints as needed, but you should only do this if you are sure of the configuration information.

Logging Logging DNS operations can be useful for monitoring and troubleshooting the DNS service. You can select different events to monitor using the properties on this tab.

FIGURE 2.6: Viewing default DNS server root hints

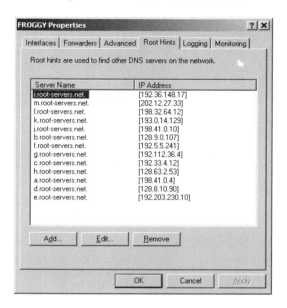

Monitoring   The Monitoring tab is useful for performing a quick check to ensure that the DNS service is operating properly. Using this tab, you will be able to perform a simple query as well as a recursive request. If both operations are successful, you can be reasonably sure that the DNS server is functioning properly.

Creating DNS Resource Records

The main functionality of a DNS server is based on the various resource records present within it. During the Active Directory installation process, you have the option of automatically configuring the DNS server for use with Active Directory. If you choose to create the default records, the resource records listed in Table 2.3 will automatically be created. Each of these records is of the type SRV (Service). The Domain and DomainTree specifiers will be based on the DNS domain name for the local domain controller, and the Site specifier will be based on your site configuration.

TABLE 2.3: Default Active Directory DNS Resource Records

Resource Record	Purpose
_ldap._tcp.*Domain*	Enumerates the domain controllers for a given domain
_ldap._tcp.*Site*.sites.*Domain*	Allows clients to find domain controllers within a specific site
_ldap._tcp.pdc.ms-dcs.*Domain*	Provides the address of the server acting as the Windows NT Primary Domain Controller (PDC) for the domain
_ldap._tcp.pdc.ms-dcs .*DomainTree*	Enumerates the global catalog servers within a domain
_ldap._tcp.S*ite*.gc.ms-dcs .*DomainTree*	Allows a client to find a global catalog server based on site configuration
_ldap._tcp.*GUID*.domains .ms-dcs.*DomainTree*	Used by computers to locate machines based on the Global Unique Identifier (GUID)
_ldap._tcp.writable .ms-dcs.*Domain*	Enumerates the domain controller(s) that hold(s) modifiable copies of the Active Directory
_ldap._tcp.*site*.sites.writable .ms-dcs.*Domain*	Enumerates domain controller(s) based on sites

In addition to the default DNS records, you will likely want to create new ones to identify specific servers and clients on your network.

DNS Interoperability

In a pure Windows 2000 environment, you would probably choose to use only Microsoft's DNS service. However, in the real world (and especially in larger environments), you might require the DNS service to interact with other implementations of DNS. A common UNIX implementation of DNS is known as the Berkeley Internet Name

Domain (BIND) service. Before you can configure various DNS server settings for interoperability, you must know which features are supported by the non-Microsoft DNS system you are using. If you want to use another vendor's DNS, make sure it is BIND release 8.1.2 or later so it supports SRV records and dynamic updates.

Interoperation with WINS and DHCP

By allowing automatic updates to DNS zones, you will be able to dramatically reduce the administrative burden of managing resource records.

To this end Microsoft's DNS can easily integrate with both Windows Internet Naming Service (WINS) and Dynamic Host Configuration Protocol (DHCP). Properly implementing and integrating these two services with DNS can help reduce administration headaches.

OVERVIEW OF DHCP

TCP/IP requires a considerable amount of manual configuration. Some of the information that might be required by a TCP/IP client in a Windows environment may include the following pieces of information:

- TCP/IP address
- Subnet mask
- Default gateway
- DNS servers
- DNS domain name
- WINS servers

Additionally, other TCP/IP services must be set. For example, if the network is using the Network Time Protocol (NTP), information on the timeserver address should also be transmitted. It's easy to see how maintaining this information even on small networks can be quite troublesome. For much larger ones, the technical and managerial issues associated with assigning appropriate information can be overwhelming. DHCP was designed to ease some of these problems. DHCP works by automatically assigning TCP/IP address information to client computers when they are first connected to the network.

If more than one DHCP server is present on the network, the client would simply take the IP address from the first one to respond. Since IP addresses are a limited resource on most networks, DHCP servers generally assign a lease duration to each IP address they assign to clients. Clients are required to renew their IP address before their lease expires, or the IP address will be retired and made available for other clients.

The pool of TCP/IP addresses available for assignment to clients is called the DHCP *scope*. A scope consists of a range of IP addresses and a subnet mask. Additionally, *scope options* can be used to specify other TCP/IP parameters, such as the default gateway, DNS servers, and WINS servers.

To provide for fault tolerance of DHCP services, a common practice is to place more than one DHCP server on the same network. However, in order to prevent any problems with duplicate IP address assignments, the DHCP servers are configured with non-overlapping address scopes.

INTEGRATING DHCP AND DNS

It doesn't take much imagination to see how DHCP information can be used to populate a DNS database. DHCP already records all of the IP address assignments within its own database. In order to reduce manual administration of DNS entries for client computers, Windows 2000's DNS implementation can automatically create Address (A) records for hosts based on DHCP information. However, the method in which DHCP information is transmitted to the DNS server varies based on the client. There are two different modes:

Windows 2000 Clients   Windows 2000 DHCP clients have the ability to automatically send updates to a dynamic DNS server as soon as they receive an IP address. This method places the task of registering the new address on the client. It also allows the client to specify whether the update of the DNS database should occur at all.

Earlier Clients   The DHCP client code for Windows 95/98 and Windows NT 4 computers does not support dynamic DNS updates.

Therefore, the DHCP server itself must update the DNS A and PTR records.

Implementing dynamic updates of DNS using information from DHCP can be done by opening the DHCP administrative tool. By right-clicking the name of the server and choosing Properties, you will have the option to select the DNS tab (see Figure 2.7).

FIGURE 2.7: Setting DNS options using the DHCP administrative tool

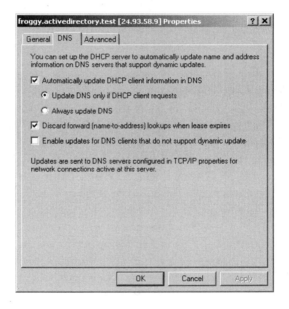

The options on this tab include the following:

Automatically Update DHCP Client Information in DNS   This option allows you to enable dynamic DNS updates from the client. This selection applies only to Windows 2000 clients. Systems administrators can choose between two options:

- The client can decide whether the update is made.

- DNS is always updated.

Discard Forward (Name-to-Address) Lookups when Lease Expires
When this option is checked, DNS entries for clients are automatically removed if a lease is not renewed in time. This is a useful option, as it will ensure outdated entries no longer exist in the DNS database.

Enable Updates for DNS Clients That Do Not Support Dynamic Update   If you have Windows NT 4, Windows 95, or Windows 98 DHCP clients and want dynamic updates of DNS, you should choose this option. When it is set, the DHCP server will be responsible for updating the DNS database whenever a new IP address is assigned.

By using the DHCP/DNS integration features of Windows 2000, you can automate what can be a very tedious process—managing client-host name-address mappings.

OVERVIEW OF WINS

Although TCP/IP has been the default base protocol since Windows NT 4, the NetBIOS protocol is heavily relied upon by versions of Windows before Windows 2000. The Windows Internet Naming Service (WINS) was designed to allow clients using NetBIOS names over the TCP/IP protocol to resolve computer names to network addresses. One of the major benefits of WINS is that it is largely self-configuring and manages itself. That is, names are added automatically to the WINS database as the server learns the addresses of clients. Although this facilitates browsing on the network, WINS has several limitations in larger environments. First, the performance of WINS can begin to degrade when many clients are registered in its database. Second, the replication functionality of the WINS database is not as robust as that of other methods (such as DNS).

With Windows 2000 and the Active Directory, Microsoft has eliminated the need for WINS altogether. However, most networks will still require the use of WINS for down-level clients (including Windows NT 4, Windows 95, and Windows 98 computers). Therefore, Windows 2000 includes an improved version of WINS. To make it easier to manage two different name-resolution methods (WINS and DNS), Windows 2000 supports automatic querying of WINS records if a host name is not found within a DNS server's database. This process, called a *WINS referral,* occurs on the server side and requires no special configuration on the client.

INTEGRATING WINS AND DNS

To enable the automatic-update process, right-click the name of a forward-lookup zone using the DNS administrative tool and select Properties. Click the WINS tab to set the dynamic update options (see Figure 2.8).

FIGURE 2.8: Setting WINS Updates

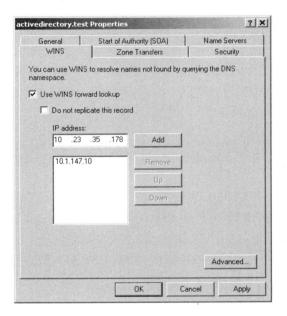

The available options include the following:

Use WINS Forward Lookup   Checking this box instructs the DNS server to query one or more WINS servers if it is unable to fulfill a host-name request. The DNS server adds a new record type—the WINS record—to its own database.

Do Not Replicate This Record   This option prevents the WINS record from being sent as part of a zone-transfer request. Therefore, the WINS records are not sent to other secondary DNS servers in the domain. You should enable this option if you are using non–Windows 2000 DNS servers on your network, as those servers will not support the WINS record type and might cause errors.

IP Address Here, you can specify the IP address(es) of the server(s) to be contacted for name resolution. If a lookup in the DNS database fails, these servers will be queried for the host-name information. Note that the order of the IP addresses matters. That is, WINS server addresses higher in the list will be contacted before those lower on the list. You can re-sort the numbers using the Up and Down buttons.

Once the preceding options are configured, the DNS server will automatically query the specified WINS servers for host names if it is not able to resolve the request within its own database. This allows both WINS and DNS clients to perform name resolution accurately while reducing administrative burdens.

In addition to WINS forward lookups, Windows 2000 DNS servers are able to perform WINS reverse lookups. The configuration options are similar and can be set by right-clicking the name of a reverse-lookup zone in the DNS administrative tool and then clicking Properties. The WINS-R tab allows you to set the WINS-R lookup information.

Necessary Procedures

Being able to install and configure Microsoft's DNS service is essential to the well-being of your Active Directory administration.

Installing the DNS Service

This procedure walks you through the steps required to install the DNS service.

1. Click Start ➤ Settings ➤ Control Panel and then double-click the Add/Remove Programs icon.

2. Select Add/Remove Windows Components.

3. Click the Components button to access a list of services and options available for installation on Windows 2000.

4. In the Windows 2000 Components Wizard, select Networking Services and then click Details.

5. Place a check mark next to the option titled Domain Name System (DNS).

Configuring DNS Zones

Once you have DNS installed, you will want to configure basic DNS zones, including a standard primary forward-lookup zone. This procedure assumes you have already installed the DNS service and no configuration options have been set.

1. Open the DNS snap-in in the Administrative Tools program group.

2. In the DNS Administration tool, right-click the name of your local server and select Configure the Server. The introduction page will inform you that the Configure DNS Server Wizard will help you configure DNS zones for this server. Click Next to begin the process.

3. Create a forward-lookup zone by choosing Yes, Create a Forward Lookup Zone, then click Next.

4. Select the type of DNS zone you want to create. The available options include Active Directory–integrated (only available if Active Directory is installed), Standard Primary, and Standard Secondary. Click Next.

5. Enter the zone name by typing in the name of the DNS zone for which you want to record addresses. For example, you might type **test.mycompany.com**. Click Next.

6. Once you have determined the name for the DNS domain, you can choose to either create a new, local DNS file or use an existing DNS file. DNS zone files are standard text files that contain mappings of IP addresses to DNS names. Usually, zone files are named as the name of the domain followed by a .DNS suffix (for example, test.mycompany.com.dns). These files must be stored in the system32/dns subdirectory of your Windows 2000 system root. Make a choice and click Next.

7. Although reverse-lookup zones are not required for basic DNS functionality and are, therefore, optional, you will probably want to create one. Reverse-lookup zones are used to map IP addresses to DNS names and are required for the proper operations of some TCP/IP applications. Select Yes, Create a Reverse Lookup Zone, and click Next.

8. Choose the reverse-lookup zone type. The options are similar to those for the forward-lookup zone. Select and click Next.

9. Specify the reverse-lookup zone. In order for reverse lookups to work properly, you must specify the network to which the zone applies. You can specify the value using a network ID or the name of the reverse-lookup zone. The value you enter will be based on the subnet(s) for which this DNS server will provide reverse-lookup information. Enter the information and click Next to continue.

10. Select a reverse-lookup zone file. Reverse-lookup zone files are created and managed similarly to forward-lookup zone files. Click Next.

11. To finalize the settings made by the Wizard, click Next. The Wizard will automatically create the forward and reverse-lookup zones based on the information you specified.

Allowing Automatic Updates

Allowing automatic updates to your DNS database will reduce administrative burden. This procedure assumes you have properly installed and configured the DNS service and have configured at least one forward-lookup zone.

1. Open the DNS snap-in in the Administrative Tools program group.

2. Expand the forward-lookup zones folder under the name of the current server.

3. Right-click the name of a zone and select Properties.

4. Change the Allow Dynamic Updates option to Yes.

5. Click OK to accept and commit the setting.

Exam Essentials

Understand DNS namespace. All names begin with the root (".") on the right-hand side. Then come top-level domains, like com, followed by second-level domains, like mycompany. The domain names are separated by a period.

Know the different DNS server roles and their functions. The DNS server roles are primary, secondary, master, and caching-only. The primary server maintains zone information. The secondary server helps offload traffic and provide fault tolerance. The master (usually a primary) server provides zone information to secondary name servers. Caching-only servers do not perform zone transfers.

Understand what a zone is and how to configure one. Zones are administrative divisions within a DNS environment. They are configured using the DNS Administration tool.

Understand the process for integrating WINS and DHCP with DNS. Both WINS and DHCP servers can help offload administrative overhead. Review these services and how they interact with DNS.

Key Terms and Concepts

caching-only DNS servers Caching-only DNS servers help resolve host names but do not participate in zone transfers.

DHCP Dynamic Host Configuration Protocol servers provide IP addressing information to clients on the network.

DNS namespace The structure of a DNS name, involving at least the root domain, top-level domain, and second-level domain.

forward-lookup zones The zone on your DNS server that contains records for all hosts on your network.

forwarding The process of having a DNS server ask another DNS server to assist in name resolution.

master DNS servers DNS servers that provide zone information to secondary DNS servers.

parent and child names A way of looking at the hierarchy of DNS names. As an example, `server1.sales.sybex.com` is a child name of the parent `sybex.com` domain name.

primary DNS server The first, and authoritative, server in a DNS zone. It holds the master copy of all zone information.

resource record (RR)   Records stored in the zone that identify the individual machines within that zone. There are different records for different machines. An example would be an MX record indicating an e-mail server.

reverse-lookup zone   DNS zone that facilitates the resolution of IP addresses to host names, as opposed to host names to IP addresses.

root domain   The root domain is represented by a period ("."). It is where all addresses on the Internet begin.

scavenging   Forcing the DNS record to be updated or discarded after a given amount of time.

secondary DNS server   DNS server designed to provide name resolution and zone fault tolerance. Secondary servers get zone information from master servers through a zone transfer.

Transmission Control Protocol/Internet Protocol (TCP/IP)   An industry-standard suite of networking protocols. The protocol used for the Internet.

WINS   Windows Internet Naming Service servers provide resolution of computer NetBIOS names to IP addresses.

zone   A logical division within a DNS domain, used for organizational or administrative purposes.

zone transfer   The process of transferring all zone information from a master DNS server to a secondary DNS server.

Sample Questions

1. Which of the following DNS names are part of the same namespace?

   A. www.microsoft.com

   B. server3.sales.microsoft.com

   C. microsoft.sybex.com

   D. publications.mktg.one.microsoft.com

Answer: A, B, and D. Answers A, B, and D all share the domain name of microsoft.com.

2. What types of DHCP clients can automatically notify the DNS server for dynamic updates?

   A. Windows 98

   B. Windows NT 4

   C. Windows for Workgroups

   D. Windows 2000

   Answer: D. Windows 2000 clients are the only ones capable of notifying the DNS server for updates.

3. What are two reasons to use a caching-only DNS server?

   A. It does not cause as much network traffic as secondary servers.

   B. It can be alone in a zone with no other DNS servers.

   C. It provides the host name to IP address resolution.

   D. It works better with BIND DNS name servers than primary servers do.

   Answer: A and C. Caching-only DNS servers provide name resolution like other types of DNS servers, but do not perform zone transfers, thereby not creating as much network traffic.

Manage, monitor, and troubleshoot DNS.

Name-resolution problems are extremely common when working with distributed networks. If you are unable to connect to a specific host name, it could be due to various reasons. First, the host itself may be unavailable if a server has gone down or if a client computer is not online. Or you may be receiving an incorrect IP address from a DNS server. Usually, the most common symptom of a DNS configuration problem is the ability to connect to a host using its IP address, but not its host name.

Critical Information

Once DNS is installed, keeping it running smoothly is central to keeping the network running properly.

Managing DNS Replication

Managing DNS replication is an important concern. If optimal settings are not chosen, you might encounter too much replication traffic. Alternatively, you might have the opposite problem—updates are not occurring frequently enough.

Monitoring DNS Servers

Know how your network services are performing at any given moment so you can determine the load on current servers, evaluate resource usage, and plan for any necessary upgrades. After you install the DNS service, you will be able to select the DNS object in the Windows 2000 Performance Monitor. This object contains many different counters related to monitoring DNS server performance and usage.

Using the Performance Monitor, you can generate statistics on the following types of events:

- Zone transfers
- DNS server memory usage
- Dynamic updates
- DNS Notify events
- Recursive queries
- TCP and UDP statistics
- WINS statistics
- Zone-transfer issues

This information can be analyzed easily using the Chart, Histogram, or Report views of the Performance Monitor. Additionally, you can use the Alerts function to automatically notify you (or other systems administrators) whenever certain performance statistic thresholds are exceeded. For example, if the total number of recursive queries is very high, you might want to be notified so you can examine the situation. Finally, information from the Performance Monitor logs can be stored to a log data file.

TIP   The Performance Monitor application in Windows 2000 is an extremely powerful and useful tool for managing and troubleshooting systems. You should become familiar with it.

Troubleshooting DNS Clients

The most common client-side problem related to DNS is incorrect TCP/IP configuration. If the DNS server address values are incorrect or the default gateway is set incorrectly, clients may not be able to contact their DNS server. Consequently, they will be unable to connect to other computers using DNS names.

One of the fundamental troubleshooting steps in diagnosing network problems is to determine whether the problem is located on the client side or server side. The most common way to find out is to see if other clients have the same problem. If, on one hand, a whole subnet is having problems resolving DNS names, it is probable that a server or network device is unavailable or improperly configured. On the other hand, if only one or a few clients are having problems, it is likely that the clients are misconfigured.

Using IPCONFIG

Many times, an error in client configuration can cause computers to unsuccessfully resolve DNS names. In this case, the client can usually connect to a machine using the machine's IP address, but not with the DNS name. The first step in troubleshooting such problems is to verify the proper TCP/IP configuration on the client. This can easily be done using the following command in Windows NT 4 or Windows 2000:

```
IPCONFIG /ALL
```

This command will list the TCP/IP configuration information for each of the client's network adapters.

NOTE The command-line parameters and output of the IPCONFIG utility is slightly different in various Microsoft operating systems. To get a listing of the exact syntax, just type **IPCONFIG /?**.

If the client computer is using DHCP, you can use the IPCONFIG /RELEASE command to release the current TCP/IP information. Then you can issue the IPCONFIG /RENEW command to obtain a new IP address lease from a DHCP server.

TIP Windows 95/98 clients have a graphical utility for viewing the same information provided by IPCONFIG. To access this utility, click Start ➤ Run, and then type **winipcfg**.

The Windows 2000 version of IPCONFIG also supports several new command-line switches in addition to those already described. These options are shown in Table 2.4.

TABLE 2.4: Windows 2000 IPCONFIG Command-Line Switches

Switch	Function
/flushdns	Clears all of the entries in the local DNS cache; useful if names are being resolved to incorrect IP addresses
/registerdns	Renews all current DHCP leases and updates DNS server information
/displaydns	Shows the contents of the current local DNS resolver cache

TABLE 2.4:   Windows 2000 IPCONFIG Command-Line Switches *(continued)*

Switch	Function
/showclassid	Shows the current DHCP class ID; used when different types of machines require specific DHCP information (for example, a different class might be used for servers and workstations)
/setclassid	Allows the current DHCP class ID to be changed

Using PING

A good second troubleshooting step is to check that the server is accessible on the network. The PING (Packet Internet Groper) command provides a simple way to do this. Simply type **PING** and then an IP address or host name at the command line.

When troubleshooting DNS problems, after running IPCONFIG to make sure TCP/IP is installed correctly, PING a machine's TCP/IP address. For example, the command PING 172.16.25.33 should return a response from a server. If no response is received, either the server is down or there is a problem with the network connectivity (such as a failed router). If, however, a response is received, you should attempt to PING a computer using its machine name. An example is PING server1.mycompany.com. If this test fails (but using PING with an IP address works), then you have a problem with your name-resolution services.

Using NSLOOKUP

Sometimes it is useful to find information about the name servers on the network. The NSLOOKUP command does just that. A basic test is to run the command with no arguments. You should see the IP address of the current DNS server for the client.

NOTE   The NSLOOKUP command is only available on Windows NT 4 and Windows 2000 machines.

The NSLOOKUP command supports many other functions for determining name-resolution paths and testing recursion. For further information, type **HELP** at the NSLOOKUP command prompt.

Unfortunately, the NSLOOKUP command is not as user-friendly as it could be. It requires you to learn several different commands and use them in a specific syntax. Nevertheless, NSLOOKUP is an invaluable tool for troubleshooting DNS configuration issues.

Troubleshooting DNS Servers

The symptoms of problems related to DNS servers generally include the inability to perform accurate name resolution. Provided the DNS server has been installed, there are some good troubleshooting steps to take:

Verify that the DNS service has started. By using the DNS administrative tool, you can quickly determine the status of the DNS server.

Check the Event Viewer. If you are having intermittent problems with the DNS server or the service has stopped unexpectedly, you can find more information in the Windows NT Event Log.

Verify that the DNS server is accessible to clients. A simple check for network connectivity between clients and the DNS server can eliminate many potential problems. Using the PING command and browsing the network and connecting to clients are two easy ways to do this. Note, however, that if name resolution is faulty, you may not be able to connect to clients.

Verify operations with NSLOOKUP. The NSLOOKUP command provides several very powerful options for testing recursion, WINS lookups, and other features of Microsoft's DNS.

Verify the DNS configuration. If the DNS server is providing inaccurate or outdated results, you may need to manually change the server settings or retire individual records. If outdated records are truly the problem, it is likely that users are able to get to many other machines (on the LAN or the Internet) but cannot connect to one or more specific computers.

If you're using implementations other than Microsoft DNS, you should consult the documentation. Although DNS is an Internet standard, various DNS-server software applications function quite differently.

Necessary Procedures

You need to know two procedures for this objective: configuring DNS replication and using NSLOOKUP.

Configuring DNS replication

In this procedure you will configure various DNS replication options. This exercise assumes that you have already created at least one DNS zone and that the local server is the primary DNS server for at least one zone.

1. Open the DNS administrative tool and expand the branch for the local server.

2. Right-click the name of a zone for which this machine is the primary server and select Properties.

3. Select the Zone Transfers tab.

4. Place a check mark in the Allow Zone Transfers box.

5. Choose whether you want to allow zone transfers from any server (the default setting), only servers specified in the Name Servers tab, or specific DNS servers based on their IP addresses. It is recommended that you choose one of the latter two options as these provide greater security.

6. Click the Notify button. Place a check mark in the Automatically Notify box. You can choose to automatically notify the servers listed on the Named Server tab, or you can specify DNS servers by IP addresses. Each of these servers will be notified automatically whenever a change to the DNS database is made.

7. Click OK twice to save the settings.

Using NSLOOKUP

In this procedure you'll use the NSLOOKUP command to verify the proper operation of the DNS server on the local machine. This exercise assumes that you have already installed and configured DNS.

1. Open a command prompt by clicking Start ➤ Programs ➤ Accessories ➤ Command Prompt. Alternatively, you can click Start ➤ Run and type **cmd.**

2. At the command prompt, type **NSLOOKUP** and press Enter. This will run the NSLOOKUP command and present you with a > prompt, which indicates that NSLOOKUP is awaiting a command.

3. To activate the local DNS server, type **Server 127.0.0.1.**

4. Type **set type = SRV** to filter resource records to only SRV types, and press Enter. If the command is successful, you will receive another > prompt.

5. To verify a resource record, simply type its FQDN. For example, if your domain name were `activedirectory.test`, you would type **ldap._tcp.activedirectory.test.** You should receive information about the host name that is mapped as a domain controller for this domain.

6. If you want to test other resources, simply type the names of the resources. You should receive valid responses. Table 2.3 provided a list of the default resource records that should be present.

7. When you are finished using NSLOOKUP, type **exit** and then press Enter. This will return you to the command prompt. To close the command prompt, type **exit** again and hit Enter.

Exam Essentials

Understand how to configure DNS zone replication.   You configure DNS zone replication by opening the DNS administration tool and going to the zone properties.

Know what PING and IPCONFIG are for. PING is for testing connectivity between machines. IPCONFIG (or WINIPCFG for 95/98 clients) shows TCP/IP configuration information.

Understand what NSLOOKUP does. NSLOOKUP can help verify the proper operation of your DNS server.

Understand proper troubleshooting procedures for possible DNS failures. First, make sure TCP/IP is installed and configured properly. Find out if the problem is with the one client or all clients. Can the client PING the IP address of the other computer? If so, does PING work using the DNS name?

Key Terms and Concepts

IPCONFIG Troubleshooting utility that displays TCP/IP configuration information on a Windows NT or Windows 2000 computer.

NSLOOKUP Diagnostic utility for DNS.

Performance Monitor Windows 2000 utility that allows you to view various performance statistics.

PING Packet Internet Groper. Used in TCP/IP environments to check connectivity between systems.

replication The process of duplicating zone information to secondary DNS servers.

WINIPCFG Shows TCP/IP-related configuration information on Windows 95/98 systems.

Sample Questions

1. You are having problems connecting to your favorite Internet site. When you PING its IP address, you get a response. However, when you PING the hostname, you do not. What is the most likely cause of the problem?

   A. The site is down.

B. Your DNS server is down.

C. The WINS server did not resolve the name properly.

D. Your DHCP server failed to notify you when the web site changed addresses.

Answer: B. The only possible answer listed above is that the DNS server is not working properly. If you did not receive a reply from PINGing the IP address, then it's possible the site is down.

2. Your boss wants to know how well the dynamic DNS update feature on your Windows 2000 DNS server is working. Which tool would you use to check its performance?

A. Network Monitor

B. NSLOOKUP

C. IPCONFIG

D. Performance Monitor

Answer: D. Performance Monitor is to be used for checking performance characteristics of computers. With Windows 2000, Performance Monitor can track, among other things, dynamic DNS updates.

Chapter

3

Installing, Configuring, Managing, Monitoring, Optimizing, and Troubleshooting Change and Configuration Management

---

MICROSOFT EXAM OBJECTIVES COVERED IN THIS CHAPTER:

Implement and troubleshoot Group Policy. *(pages 107 – 122)*

- Create a Group Policy Object (GPO).
- Link an existing GPO.
- Delegate administrative control of Group Policy.
- Modify Group Policy inheritance.
- Filter Group Policy settings by associating security groups to GPOs.
- Modify Group Policy.

Manage and troubleshoot user environments by using Group Policy. *(pages 122 – 128)*

- Control user environments by using administrative templates.
- Assign script policies to users and computers.

Manage network configuration by using Group Policy. *(pages 128 – 131)*

▶ **Manage and troubleshoot software by using Group Policy.** *(pages 131 – 148)*

- Deploy software by using Group Policy.

- Maintain software by using Group Policy.

- Configure deployment options.

- Troubleshoot common problems that occur during software deployment.

▶ **Deploy Windows 2000 by using Remote Installation Services (RIS).** *(pages 148 – 169)*

- Install an image on a RIS client computer.

- Create a RIS boot disk.

- Configure remote-installation options.

- Troubleshoot RIS problems.

- Manage images for performing remote installations.

▶ **Configure RIS security.** *(pages 169 – 175)*

- Authorize a RIS server.

- Grant computer account creation rights.

- Prestage RIS client computers for added security and load balancing.

Windows 2000 provides a flexibly secure network operating environment. One of the easiest ways to employ required security measures is to implement Group Policies. Group Policies are used for simple tasks such as limiting access to a resource, but are also available for complex procedures like deploying and maintaining software. Through a Group Policy Object, you could give a set of employees access to a certain database; another Group Policy can prohibit the group from editing the Registry.

Another nice feature of Windows 2000 is the ability to remotely install client machines. Through Remote Installation Services, or RIS, you can easily install clients and ensure each gets the proper software.

▶ Implement and troubleshoot Group Policy.

One of the biggest challenges faced by systems administrators is the management of users, groups, and client computers. It's difficult enough to deploy and manage workstations throughout the environment. When you consider that users are generally able to make system-configuration changes, it can quickly become a management nightmare!

Windows 2000 provides a solution that's readily available and easy to implement: *Group Policy*. Through the use of *Group Policy Objects (GPOs)*, you can quickly and easily define restrictions on common actions and then apply these at the site, domain, or organizational-unit (OU) level.

Critical Information

Windows 2000's Group Policies are designed to allow you to customize user settings and place restrictions on the actions users can perform. Group Policies can be easily created and later applied to one or more users or computers within the environment. Using Group Policies is much more efficient than manually editing the Registry. Group Policy settings can be managed from within the Active Directory environment, utilizing the structure of users, groups, and OUs.

Group Policy Settings

Group Policy settings are based on Group Policy *administrative templates*, which provide a list of user-friendly configuration options and specify the system settings to which they apply. When configuration options are set, the appropriate change is made in the Registry of the designated user(s) and computer(s).

Windows 2000 comes with several Administrative Template files for managing common settings. Additionally, you can create your own Administrative Template files to set options for specific functionality.

Most Group Policy items have three setting options:

Enabled Specifies that a setting for this Group Policy object has been configured. Some settings will require values or options to be set.

Disabled Indicates the chosen option is disabled for client computers. Disabling an option *is* a setting, because it specifies you want to disallow certain functionality.

Not Configured Specifies that these settings have been neither enabled nor disabled. Not Configured is the default option for most settings. It simply states this Group Policy will not specify an option and settings from other policy settings may take precedence. This setting has the benefit of not adding to the size of the Registry hive transmitted to the client, thereby saving bandwidth.

The specific options available (and their effects) will depend on the setting. Often, additional information is required. For example, when setting the Account Lockout policy, you must specify how many bad login attempts may be made before the account is locked out.

User and Computer Settings

Group Policy settings can apply to two types of Active Directory objects: users and computers. Since both users and computers can be placed into groups and organized within OUs, this type of configuration simplifies the management of hundreds or even thousands of computers.

The main settings that can be made within User and Computer Group Policies are:

Software Settings   Software settings apply to specific applications installed on the computer. You can use these settings to make new applications available to end users and control the default configuration for these applications.

Windows Settings   Windows-settings options allow you to customize the behavior of the Windows operating system. The specific options available here differ for users and computers. For example, user-specific settings allow the configuration of Internet Explorer (including the default home page and other settings), whereas computer settings include security options such as account policy and event-log options.

Administrative Templates   The options available in Administrative Templates are used to further configure user and computer settings. In addition to the default options available, you can create your own administrative templates with custom options.

Figure 3.1 provides an example of the types of options that can be configured with Group Policy.

FIGURE 3.1:   Group Policy configuration options

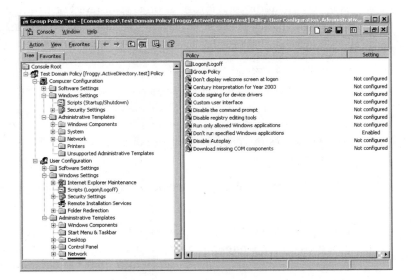

Group Policy Objects

For ease of management, Group Policies may be contained in items called Group Policy Objects (GPOs). GPOs act as containers for the settings made within Group Policy files. For example, you might have different policies for users and computers in different departments. Based on these requirements, you could create a GPO for members of the Sales department and another for members of the Engineering department. Then you could apply the GPOs to the OU for each department.

Group Policy settings are hierarchical; they can be applied at three different levels:

Sites   GPOs can be configured to apply to entire sites within an Active Directory environment. The settings apply to all of the site's domains and severs and are useful when you want to make settings apply to all of the domains within an Active Directory tree or forest.

Domains   GPO settings placed at this level will only apply to all of the user and computer objects within the domain.

NOTE   Typically, GPO master settings are made at the domain level.

Organizational Units   The lowest level of settings for GPOs is at the OU level. By configuring Group Policy options for OUs, you can take advantage of the hierarchical structure of the Active Directory. If the OU structure is planned well, it will be easy to make logical GPO assignments for various business units at the OU level.

You can set up Group Policy settings at any or all of these three levels. Because the settings are cumulative by default, a User object might receive policy settings from the site level, domain level, and organizational units in which it is contained.

Inheritance

In most cases, Group Policy settings for an object are cumulative based on inheritance from their parent containers. What happens if settings conflict? By default, settings at the most specific level will override those at more general levels.

Although the default is for settings to be cumulative and inherited, you can modify this. Two main options can be set at the various levels to which GPOs might apply:

Block Policy Inheritance   Block Policy Inheritance specifies that Group Policy settings for an object are not inherited from its parents.

WARNING   Blocking policy inheritance should be managed carefully, because it allows other systems administrators to override the settings made at higher levels.

Force Policy Inheritance   Force Policy Inheritance can be placed on a parent object and ensures that all lower-level objects inherit these settings. This will override blocking policy inheritance.

Forcing policy inheritance is used when you want to globally enforce a specific setting. For example, if a password expiration policy should apply to all users and computers within a domain, you could create a

GPO with the Force Policy Inheritance option enabled at the domain level.

If there is a conflict between the computer and user settings, the user settings will take effect, because the user settings are more specific.

TIP Be prepared for questions concerning inheritance on the exam.

Creating GPOs

Although only one Group Policy editing application is included with Windows 2000, you can access it several ways, as systems administrators may choose to apply the Group Policy settings at different levels within the Active Directory. In order to create GPOs at different levels, you can use the following tools:

Active Directory Sites and Services Used for linking GPOs at the site level.

Active Directory Users and Computers Used for linking GPOs at the domain or OU level.

MMC Group Policy Snap-In By directly configuring the Microsoft Management Console (MMC) Group Policy snap-in, you can access and edit GPOs at any level of hierarchy. The snap-in also allows you to modify the local Group Policy settings and create a custom console saved to the Administrative Tools program group.

WARNING Be careful when making Group Policy settings, because certain options might prevent the proper use of systems on your network. Always test Group Policy settings on a small group of users before deploying GPOs throughout your organization.

Linking and Testing GPOs

Creating GPOs is the first step in assigning Group Policies. The second step is to link the GPO to a specific Active Directory object. GPOs can be linked to sites, domains, and OUs.

The Active Directory Users and Computers tool offers much flexibility for assigning GPOs. You can create new GPOs, add multiple GPOs, edit them directly, change priority settings, remove links, and delete GPOs all from within this interface. Creating new GPOs using Active Directory Sites and Services or Active Directory Users and Computers is usually the quickest and easiest way to create the settings you need.

To test the Group Policy settings, create a user or computer account within a Group Policy OU. Then, using another computer that is a member of the same domain, log on as the newly created user. You should notice the changes.

Filtering Group Policy

To secure administrative access to GPOs or to enable or disable their application at the client level, you can set permissions on the GPOs themselves. First, select the Group Policy tab for an object with the GPO assigned and then click Properties. By clicking the Security tab, you can view the specific permissions set on the GPO (see Figure 3.2).

FIGURE 3.2: GPO security settings

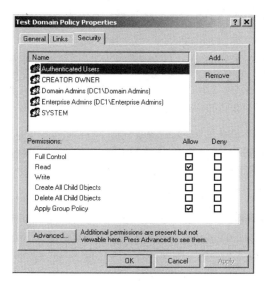

WARNING Do not grant users Full Control or Write ability to their GPO, unless you really want them making their own security decisions.

The Apply Group Policy setting is particularly important because it is used for filtering the scope of the GPO. *Filtering* is the process by which selected security groups are included or excluded from the effects of the GPOs. To specify that the settings should apply to a GPO, you should grant at least the Apply Group Policy and Read settings. These settings will only be applied if the security group is also contained within a site, domain, or OU to which the GPO is linked. In order to disable GPO access for a group, choose Deny for both settings. Finally, if you do not want to specify either Allow or Deny effects, leave both boxes blank—it is effectively the same as having no setting.

TIP To have the GPO in effect for a group, you Allow the Apply Group Policy for that group.

Delegating Administrative Control of GPOs

You must establish the appropriate security on GPOs for two reasons. First, if the security settings aren't set properly, users and systems administrators can easily override them. Second, having many different systems administrators creating and modifying GPOs can cause settings that may violate security or company policies.

Determining security permissions for GPOs is done through the Delegation of Control Wizard. Specifically, the process involves delegating the ability to manage Group Policy links on an Active Directory object, such as an OU.

Controlling Group Policy Inheritance

By default, GPO settings flow from higher-level Active Directory objects to lower-level ones. The effective set of Group Policy settings for a user might be based on GPOs assigned at the site level, the domain level, and in the OU hierarchy.

However, you might want to block Group Policy inheritance by selecting the properties for the object to which a GPO has been linked. On the Group Policy tab, you will be able to set several useful options regarding inheritance. The first option is the Block Policy Inheritance check box located at the bottom of the Group Policy tab (see Figure 3.3). By enabling this option, you establish that this object starts with a clean slate. No other Group Policy settings will apply to the contents of this Active Directory site, domain, or OU.

FIGURE 3.3: Blocking GPO inheritance

You can, however, force inheritance. The No Override option is generally set to prevent other systems administrators from making changes to default policies. You can set the No Override option by clicking the Options button in the Group Policy tab for the object to which the GPO applies. You can also temporarily disable a GPO, which is useful during troubleshooting and when attempting to determine which GPOs are causing a certain behavior.

Troubleshooting Group Policy

One potential problem with GPO configuration is sluggish logons and system startups. It is especially problematic in large environments when Group Policy settings must be transmitted over the network and, in many cases, slow WAN links. You should limit the number of GPOs because of the processing overhead and network requirements during logon. By default, GPOs are processed in a synchronous manner, i.e., one GPO processing must be completed before another (as opposed to asynchronous processing, where all execute simultaneously).

Another common problem is unexpected settings of Group Policy options. When this occurs, you should verify the following options:

Locate Active Directory GPO Links   To find out where GPOs are being used, you can use the Links tab in the properties of the GPO.

Verify GPO Configuration   Since GPOs can be assigned to sites, domains, and OUs, you should carefully plan for the inheritance of Group Policy settings. While careful planning and maintenance of GPOs is important, it's just as important to determine the ramifications of moving and reconfiguring objects of the Active Directory. For example, moving an OU or redefining a site can trigger many changes in the effective Group Policy settings.

Attempt to "Disable" Certain GPOs   When certain settings are causing problems, it can be difficult to isolate the related GPOs. One method for troubleshooting GPO problems is to systematically disable and enable various combinations of GPOs. Thus, you can determine which GPO(s) is causing the problems.

TIP   A scenario involving troubleshooting Group Policies could make a great test question.

Necessary Procedures

There are four necessary procedures for this objective you need to know how to perform: Creating a GPO, Linking a GPO, Filtering Group Policy, and Delegating Administrative Control for a Group Policy.

Creating a Group Policy Object Using MMC

Create a custom Group Policy snap-in for managing user and computer settings.

1. Click Start ➤ Run, type **mmc**, and press Enter.

2. On the Console menu, click Add/Remove Snap-In.

3. Click the Add button. Select Group Policy from the list, and click Add.

4. For the Group Policy Object setting, click Browse. Note that you can set the scope to Domains/OUs, Sites, or Computers. On the Domains/OUs tab, click the New Policy button (located to the right of the Look In drop-down list).

5. To name the new object, type the name. Click OK to open the Policy object.

6. Place a check mark next to the Allow the Focus of the Group Policy Snap-In to Be Changed When Launching from the Command Line option. This will allow the context of the snap-in to be changed when you launch the MMC item.

7. Click Finish to create the Group Policy Object. Click Close on the Add Standalone Snap-In dialog box. Finally, click OK to add the new snap-in.

8. You can make changes to default settings for this new GPO. Open the following items: the name of the Group Policy Object ➤ Computer Configuration ➤ Windows Settings ➤ Security Settings ➤ Local Policies ➤ Security Options.

9. Double-click the Do Not Display Last User Name in Logon Screen option. Place a check mark next to the Define This Policy Setting in the Template option, and then select Enabled. Click OK to save the setting.

10. Double-click the Message Title for Users Attempting to Log On option. Place a check mark next to the Define This Policy Setting in the Template option and then type a policy statement to be read by users. Click OK to save the setting.

11. Now, to make changes to the User settings, expand the following objects: the name of the Group Policy Object ➤ User Configuration ➤ Administrative Templates ➤ Start Menu & Task Bar.

12. Double-click the Add Logoff to the Start Menu option. Note that you can get a description of the purpose of this setting by clicking the Explain tab. Select Enabled and then click OK.

13. Expand the following objects: the name of the Group Policy Object ➤ User Configuration ➤ Administrative Templates ➤ System.

14. Double-click the Don't Run Specified Windows Applications option. Select Enabled, and then click the Show button. To add to the list of disallowed applications, click the Add button. When prompted to enter the item, type the name of an application, like **wordpad.exe**. To save the setting, click OK three times.

15. To change network configuration settings, click the name of the Group Policy Object ➤ User Configuration ➤ Administrative Templates ➤ Network ➤ Offline Files. Note that you can change the default file locations for several different network folders.

16. To change script settings (which we will cover later in this chapter), click the name of the Group Policy Object ➤ Computer Configuration ➤ Windows Settings ➤ Scripts (Startup/Shutdown). Note that you can add script settings by double-clicking either the Startup and/or Shutdown item.

17. The changes you have made for this GPO are automatically saved. You can optionally save this customized MMC console by selecting Save As from the Console menu. Then, provide a name for the new MMC snap-in (such as "Group Policy Test"). You will now see this item in the Administrative Tools program group.

18. When you are finished modifying the Group Policy settings, close the MMC tool.

Linking GPOs to the Active Directory

In this procedure you will link the GPO to an OU. This procedure assumes you completed the previous procedure.

1. Open the Active Directory Users and Computers tool.

2. Create a new top-level OU, giving it a name.

3. Right-click the OU and click Properties.

4. Select the Group Policy tab. To add a new policy at the OU level, click Add. In the Look In drop-down list, select the name of the local domain. Select the name of the GPO and then click OK.

5. Note that you can also add additional GPOs to this OU. When multiple GPOs are assigned, you can also control the order in which they apply by using the Up and Down buttons. Finally, you can edit the GPO by clicking the Edit button, and you can remove the link (or, optionally, delete the GPO entirely) by clicking the Delete button.

6. To save the GPO link, click OK. When finished, close the Active Directory Users and Computers tool.

Filtering Group Policy Using Security Groups

In this procedure you will filter Group Policy using security groups. In order to complete this procedure, you must have completed the previous two procedures.

1. Open the Active Directory Users and Computers administrative tool.

2. Create two new Global Security groups within the OU previously created and name them.

3. Right-click the OU and select Properties. Select the Group Policy tab.

4. Highlight GPO and select Properties.

5. On the Security tab, click Add and select the two new groups. Click OK.

6. Highlight the first group and select Deny for the Read and Apply Group Policy permissions. The specification will prevent users in this group from being affected by the policy.

7. Highlight the other group and select Allow for the Read and Apply Group Policy permissions. Users in this group will be affected by this policy.

8. Click OK to save the Group Policy settings. You will be warned that Deny takes precedence over any other security settings. Select Yes to continue.

9. Click OK to save the change to the properties of the OU.

10. When finished, close the Active Directory Users and Computers administrative tool.

Delegating Administrative Control of Group Policy

In this procedure you will delegate permissions to manage Group Policies of an OU. In order to perform these steps, you must have first completed the first two procedures in this section.

1. Open the Active Directory Users and Computers tool.

2. Expand the local domain and create and name a user within the OU.

3. Right-click the OU and select Delegate Control.

4. Click Next to start the Delegation of Control Wizard.

5. On the Users or Groups page, click Add. Select the account and click OK. Click Next to continue.

6. On the Tasks to Delegate step, select Delegate the Following Common Tasks and place a check mark next to the Manage Group Policy Links item. Click Next to continue.

7. Finally, click Finish to complete the Delegation of Control Wizard and assign the appropriate permissions. Specifically, this will allow the user to create GPO links to this OU (and, by default, any child OUs).

8. When finished, close the Active Directory Users and Computers tool.

Exam Essentials

Understand what a Group Policy Object is.   Group policies allow you to define restrictions on common actions and then apply these at the site, domain, or organizational-unit (OU) level.

Know what linking a GPO to a site, domain, or OU does.   Linking a GPO to a site, domain, or OU allows you to determine who is going to be affected by that GPO. Linking a GPO to a site may allow you to affect many more users than linking it to an OU.

Understand what filtering is.   Filtering is the process by which selected security groups are included or excluded from the effects of the GPOs.

Know how GPO inheritance works.   By default, GPO settings flow from higher-level Active Directory objects to lower-level ones. Inheritance can be both forced to lower-level objects and blocked from higher-level objects.

Key Terms and Concepts

administrative templates   Allow for the creation of custom settings within Group Policy Objects.

filtering   The process by which selected security groups are included or excluded from the effects of the GPOs.

GPO link   Connection between a GPO and the Active Directory object it is intended to affect.

Group Policy   System settings that allow or disallow certain actions to be performed by groups of users.

Group Policy Objects (GPOs)   Containers for the settings made within Group Policy files.

inheritance   Process where GPO settings flow from a higher-level Active Directory object to a lower-level Active Directory object.

Sample Questions

1. To enable GPO settings for a specific security group, which of the following permissions should be applied?

A. Deny Read

B. Allow Read

C. Enable Apply Group Policy

D. Disable Apply Group Policy

E. Both A and D

F. Both B and C

Answer: F. To enable the application of Group Policy on a security group, both the Read and Apply Group Policy options should be enabled.

2. GPOs assigned at which of the following levels will override GPO settings at the site level?

A. OU

B. Site

C. Domain

D. Both OU and domain

E. None of the above

Answer: D. GPOs at the OU level take precedence over GPOs at the domain level. GPOs at the domain level, in turn, take precedence over GPOs at the site level.

Manage and troubleshoot user environments by using Group Policy.

Once you have implemented GPOs and applied them to sites, domains, and OUs within the Active Directory, it's time to manage them. Proper management of Group Policy can greatly reduce the time the help desk spends troubleshooting common problems.

Critical Information

One of the main reasons for using Group Policies is to configure users' environments. Although Microsoft has included many of the most common and useful items by default, they have also made it possible for you to create and include your own templates.

Using Administrative Templates

Microsoft's default Policy settings are made available when you create new GPOs or edit existing ones. Creating your own templates and including them in the list of settings allows you to further customize your users' environments.

Several templates are included with Windows 2000:

Common.adm   Contains the policy options common to both Windows 95/98 and Windows NT 4 computers.

Inetres.adm   Contains the policy options for configuring Internet Explorer options on Windows 2000 client computers.

System.adm   Includes common configuration options and settings for Windows 2000 client computers.

Windows.adm   Contains policy options for Windows 95/98 computers.

Winnt.adm   Contains policy options that are specific to the use of Windows NT 4.

These Administrative Template files are stored within the inf subdirectory of the system root directory. Note that the use of the Windows.adm, Winnt.adm, and Common.adm files is not supported in Windows 2000. These files are provided for backward compatibility with previous versions of Windows.

The *.adm files are text files that follow a specific format recognized by the Group Policy editor. If necessary, you can create custom Administrative Template files that include more options for configuration.

To add new administrative templates when modifying GPOs, simply right-click the Administrative Templates object and select Add/Remove Templates (see Figure 3.4).

FIGURE 3.4: Adding administrative templates when creating GPOs

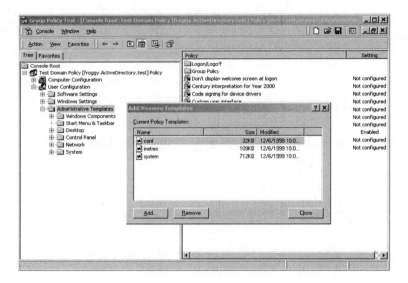

Assigning Script Policies

Script policies are specific options that are part of Group Policy settings for users and computers. These settings direct the operating system to specific files that should be processed during the startup/shutdown or logon/logoff processes. Perhaps the most common operation for logon scripts is mapping network drives. Although users can manually map network drives, providing this functionality within login scripts ensures that mappings stay consistent and that users need only remember the drive letters for their resources.

The scripts may be created through *Windows Script Host (WSH)* or standard batch file commands. WSH is a utility included with the Windows 2000 operating system that presents a runtime environment to parse and execute scripts. It allows developers and systems administrators to create scripts using the familiar Visual Basic Scripting Edition (VBScript) or JScript (Microsoft's implementation of JavaScript). Additionally, WSH can be expanded to accommodate other common scripting languages.

To set script-policy options, you simply edit the Group Policy settings. As shown in Figure 3.5, there are two main areas for setting script policy settings:

Startup/Shutdown Scripts   Settings for Startup/Shutdown scripts are located within the Computer Configuration ➢ Windows Settings ➢ Scripts (Startup/Shutdown) object.

Logon/Logoff Scripts   Logon/Logoff script settings are located within the User Configuration ➢ Windows Settings ➢ Scripts (Logon/Logoff) object.

FIGURE 3.5: Viewing script policy settings

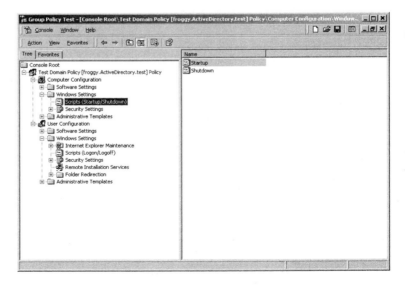

To assign scripts, simply double-click the setting. The Startup Properties dialog box appears, as shown in Figure 3.6. To add a script filename, click the Add button. You will be asked to provide the name of the script file (such as MapNetworkDrives.vbs or ResetEnvironment.bat).

FIGURE 3.6: Setting scripting options

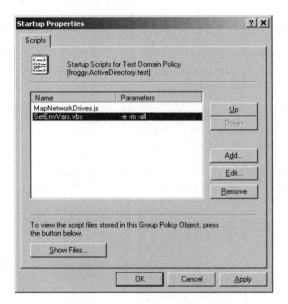

NOTE You can change the order in which the scripts are run by using the Up and Down buttons.

The Show Files button will open the directory folder in which you should store the Logon files.

TIP Place the files within the Sysvol share so that the files are replicated to all domain controllers.

Necessary Procedures

For a better understanding of this objective, you should use the Group Policy editor to open the various *.adm files and examine their contents.

Exam Essentials

Understand how to manage user environments with Group Policies. Administrative templates can be used for specifying settings that may otherwise not be available using Group Policies. Script policies and the Windows Scripting Host allow you to even further customize your users' environment.

Key Terms and Concepts

administrative templates Allow for the creation of custom settings within Group Policy Objects.

script policies Used for making changes during the startup of a computer or during the logon for a user.

Windows Script Host (WSH) Tool used for the creation of a runtime environment that supports the parsing and execution of scripted policies.

Sample Questions

1. Script policies can be written in which of the following languages?

A. Visual Basic Scripting Edition (VBScript)

B. JScript

C. Other Windows Script Host (WSH) languages

D. Batch files

E. All of the above

Answer: E. The Windows Script Host (WSH) can be used with any of the above languages.

2. In order to be accessible to other domain controllers, logon/logoff and startup/shutdown scripts should be placed in which of the following shares?

A. Winnt

B. System

C. C$

D. Sysvol

E. None of the above

Answer: D. By default, the contents of the Sysvol share are made available to all domain controllers. Therefore, scripts should be placed in these directories.

Manage network configuration by using Group Policy.

Although many different methods exist for handling network settings at the protocol level (such as Dynamic Host Configuration Protocol, or DHCP), Group Policy allows administrators to set which functions and operations are available to users and computers.

Critical Information

Figure 3.7 shows some available features for managing a user's network configuration through Group Policy settings. You can manage network configuration on a computer level as well. The paths to these settings are as follows:

Computer Network Options You may find computer network options settings within the Computer Configuration ➢ Administrative Templates ➢ Network folder.

User Network Options   Look under the User Configuration ➤ Administrative Templates ➤ Network folder to locate user network options settings.

FIGURE 3.7: Viewing Group Policy user network configuration options

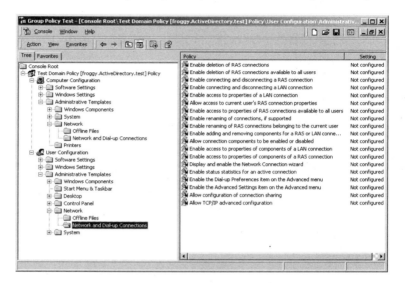

Here are some examples of the types of settings available:

- The ability to allow or disallow the modification of network settings. In many environments, the improper changing of network configurations and protocol settings is a common cause of help-desk calls.

- The ability to allow or disallow the creation of Remote Access Service (RAS) connections. This option is very useful, especially in larger networked environments, because the use of modems and other WAN devices can pose a security threat to the network.

- Offline files and folders options, especially useful for keeping files synchronized for traveling users and commonly configured for laptops.

Necessary Procedures

Even though this objective is short on substance, it is long on practicality. You will want to know where to configure networking options using Group Policies.

Examining Group Policy Networking Options

Open the Group Policy object you created during the first procedure for this chapter. Once inside, familiarize yourself with the networking options:

- Computer Network Options, located within the Computer Configuration ➤ Administrative Templates ➤ Network folder.

- User Network Options, located within the User Configuration ➤ Administrative Templates ➤ Network folder.

Exam Essentials

Understand how to modify Group Policies to include specific network settings. Use the Group Policy snap-in from the MMC. Open your policy and choose either Computer Configuration or User Configuration ➤ Administrative Templates ➤ Network folder.

Key Terms and Concepts

Dynamic Host Configuration Protocol Protocol and service that automatically assigns client-side TCP/IP configuration information.

Sample Questions

1. Which networking options can users be blocked from modifying by using Group Policies?

    A. IP address

    B. Subnet mask

C. Domain name

D. All of the above

Answer: D. Group Policies can (and likely should) block users from modifying any of their network settings.

Manage and troubleshoot software by using Group Policy.

Although the proper configuration of the Active Directory and client and server operating systems is very important, the real power of the computer for end users is in the applications they use. Windows 2000 and the Active Directory provide many improvements to the old, manual processes of deploying and managing software. Through the use of Group Policy objects and the Microsoft Installer (MSI), software deployment options can be easily configured.

Critical Information

When installing software in network environments, there are three main steps:

- First and foremost, you must determine which applications specific users require.

- Second, the IT department must purchase the appropriate licenses for the software and acquire any necessary media.

- The fun part is third—actually installing the applications on users' machines. Whether you have the end users install it themselves or dedicate valuable IT staff time to accomplish this, there are several possible problems. The main two are inconsistency in installation and lost productivity from downtime.

One of the key design goals for the Active Directory was to reduce the headaches involved in managing software and configurations in a networked environment. Windows 2000 offers several features that can make the task of deploying software easier and less prone to errors.

The Windows Installer

Because of the many problems associated with traditional software installation, Microsoft created a new component that supports a clearly defined and enforced standard for managing the installation process. Windows Installer provides for better manageability of installation and gives you more control over deployment. The benefits to using the Windows Installer are:

Improved Software Removal   Remnants left behind during the uninstall process can eventually clutter up the Registry and file system. During installation, the Windows Installer keeps track of all of the changes made. When it comes time to remove an application, all these changes can then be rolled back.

More Robust Installation Routines   If a typical setup program is aborted during software installation, the results are unpredictable. The Windows Installer allows you to roll back any changes when the application setup is aborted.

Ability to Use Elevated Privileges   Application installation usually requires Administrator permissions on the local computer. Windows Installer is able to employ temporarily elevated privileges so users, regardless of their security settings, can install authorized applications.

Support for Repairing Corrupted Applications   Regardless of how well a network environment is managed, critical files are sometimes lost or corrupted. *Windows Installer packages* allow you to verify the installation of an application and replace any missing or corrupted files.

Prevention of File Conflicts   Different versions of the same files should be compatible with each other. In the real world, you know better. Windows Installer accurately tracks which files are used by certain programs and ensures that any shared files are not improperly deleted or overwritten.

Automated Installations   Typical application setup processes require responses to several prompts. By using the Windows Installer, however, you can specify setup options before the process begins.

Advertising and On-Demand Installations   One of the most powerful features of the Windows Installer is its ability to perform on-demand installations of software. The Windows Installer supports a function known as *advertising*. Advertising makes applications appear to be available via the Start menu. However, the programs themselves may not actually be installed on the system. When a user attempts to access an advertised application, the Windows Installer automatically downloads the necessary files from a server and installs the program.

Windows Installer File Types

When performing software deployment with the Windows Installer in Windows 2000, you may encounter several different file types:

Windows Installer Packages (.MSI)   In order to take full advantage of Windows Installer functionality, applications must include Windows Installer packages, which hold specific installation and configuration information and are normally created by third-party application vendors and software developers.

Transformation Files (.MST)   *Transformation files* are useful when customizing installation. When you choose to assign or publish an application, you may want to specify additional options for the package, like allowing only Word and Excel to be installed from the Office suite.

Patches (.MSP)   In order to maintain software, *patches* are often required. Patches may make minor Registry and/or file system changes and are subject to certain limitations.

Initialization Files (.ZAP)   In order to provide support for publishing non–Windows Installer applications, *initialization files* can be used. These files provide links to a standard executable file used to install an application. An example of an executable file might be \\server1\software\program1\setup.exe. Once initialization files are published or advertised, users can access the *Add/Remove Programs* icon to install them over the network.

Application Assignment Scripts (.AAS)   *Application assignment scripts* store information regarding the assignment of programs and any settings made by the systems administrator. These files are created when Group Policy is used to create software package assignments for users and computers.

Windows Installer Settings

Several options, which can be set within a GPO, influence the behavior of the Windows Installer. The options are accessed by navigating to User Configuration ➤ Administrative Templates ➤ Windows Components ➤ Windows Installer. The options are:

Always Install with Elevated Privileges   This policy allows users to install applications that require elevated privileges. For example, if a user does not have the permissions necessary to modify the Registry, but the installation program must make Registry changes, this policy will allow the process to succeed.

Search Order   This setting specifies the order in which the Windows Installer will search for installation files. The options include n (for network shares), m (for searching removable media), and u (for searching the Internet for installation files).

Disable Rollback   When this option is enabled, the Windows Installer does not store the system-state information required to roll back the installation of an application. Disable Rollback reduces the amount of temporary disk space required during installation and increases installation performance. However, the drawback is the system cannot roll back to its original state if the installation fails and the application needs to be removed.

Disable Media Source for Any Install   This option disallows the installation of software using removable media (such as CD-ROM, DVD, or floppy diskettes).

Preparing for Software Deployment

Before you can install applications on client computers, you must make sure the necessary files are available to end users. To do this, you create shares on file servers that include the installation files for many applications.

TIP   Know how to create a share under Windows 2000.

Once you have created an application distribution share, it's time to publish and assign the applications.

Assigning and Publishing Applications

Two main methods, *assigning* and *publishing,* make programs available to clients using the Active Directory. The various settings for assigned and published applications are managed through the use of Group Policy Objects (GPOs): You create a GPO that includes software deployment settings for users and computers and link it to the appropriate Active Directory objects.

Assigning Applications

Software applications can be assigned to users and computers, making the programs available for automatic installation. The applications advertise their availability to the affected users or computers by placing icons within the Programs folder of the Start menu.

When applications are assigned to a user, the programs will be advertised to that user regardless of which computer is utilized. If the user starts a program not yet installed on the local computer, the application will automatically be installed on the computer from a server.

When an application is assigned to a computer, the program is made available to any users of the computer. If the application was not installed, the user attempting to run it for the first time would be prompted for required setup information.

Generally, widely used applications should be assigned to computers. Any applications used by only a few users (or those with specific job tasks) should be assigned to users.

Publishing Applications

When applications are published, the programs are advertised, but no icons are automatically created. Instead, the applications are made available for installation using the *Add/Remove Programs* icon in the Control Panel. Software can be published only to users (not computers). The list of available applications is stored within the Active Directory, and users can query this list when they need to install programs. For ease of organization, applications can be grouped into *categories*.

When software installation categories have been created, users opening the Add/Remove Programs item in the Control Panel and choosing Add New Programs will see several options in the Category drop-down list. The applications will be listed under the appropriate category you created.

TIP   Be familiar with the differences between assigning and publishing applications.

Verifying Software Installation

In order to ensure that the settings you made in the GPO have taken place, you can log in to the domain from a Windows 2000 Professional computer within the OU to which the settings apply. The icons for any applications you assigned should show up, and any published applications should appear under Add/Remove Programs in Control Panel. The real test is in performing the installation.

Configuring Software Deployment Settings

In addition to the basic operations of assigning and publishing applications, several other options exist for specifying the details of how software is deployed. You can access these options from within a GPO by right-clicking the Software Installation item, located within Software Settings in User Configuration or Computer Configuration.

Managing Package Defaults

In the General tab of the Software Installation Properties dialog box, you'll be able to specify some defaults for any packages you create within the particular GPO. Figure 3.8 shows the General options for managing software-installation settings.

FIGURE 3.8: General settings for software properties

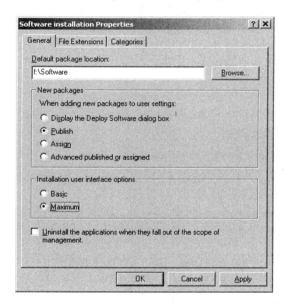

The General options are:

Default Package Location   Default Package Location specifies the default file system or network location for software-installation packages.

New Packages Options   The setting indicates the default type of package assignment to be used when adding a new package to either the user or computer settings. If you'll be assigning or publishing multiple packages, it may be useful to set a default here.

Installation User Interface Options   It may or may not be desirable for users at installation to see the advanced installation options. If Basic is chosen, the user will only be able to configure the minimal settings (such as the installation location). If Maximum is chosen, all of the available installation options will be displayed. The specific installation options available will depend on the package.

Uninstall the Applications When They Fall Out of the Scope of Management   What happens when effective GPOs change? Suppose User A is currently located within the Sales OU. A GPO that assigns the Microsoft Office 2000 suite of applications is linked to the Sales OU. You decide to move User A to the Engineering OU, which has no software deployment settings. Should the application be uninstalled, or should it remain? If the Uninstall the Applications When They Fall Out of the Scope of Management option is checked, applications will be removed if not specifically assigned or published within GPOs.

Managing File Extension Mappings

One of the potential problems associated with the use of many different file types is it's difficult to keep track of which applications work with which files. Through software deployment settings, you can specify mappings for specific *file extensions*. For example, you could specify that whenever users attempt to access a file with the extension .VSD, the operating system should attempt to open the file using Visio diagramming software. If Visio is not installed on the user's machine, the computer could automatically download and install it (assuming the application has been properly advertised). This method allows users to have applications automatically installed when needed.

Such results from mappings can occur without further interaction with the user. You can manage file-extension mappings by viewing the properties for any package you have defined within the Group Policy settings. Figure 3.9 shows how file-extension settings can be managed. The list of file extensions you'll see is based on the specific software packages in the GPO.

FIGURE 3.9: Managing file extensions

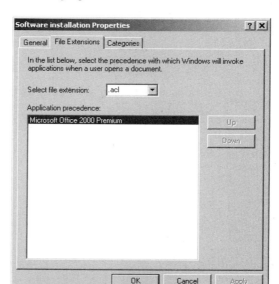

Creating Application Categories

In your network you may have hundreds of published applications. Users looking for one specific program may find the search daunting.

Creating categories reduces the hassle. You can manage the application categories for users and computers by right-clicking the Software Installation item, selecting Properties, and clicking the Categories tab. Figure 3.10 shows you how application categories can be created.

FIGURE 3.10: Creating application categories

Once created, you can view the software-installation categories by opening the Add/Remove Programs item in the Control Panel. When you click Add New Programs, you'll see several options in the Category drop-down list. When you select the properties for a package, you will be able to assign the application to one or more of the categories.

Removing Programs

An important phase in the software-management life cycle is the removal of applications. The Active Directory and Windows Installer can easily remove programs. To that end, right-click the package within the Group Policy settings and select All Tasks ➤ Remove (see Figure 3.11).

FIGURE 3.11: Removing a software package

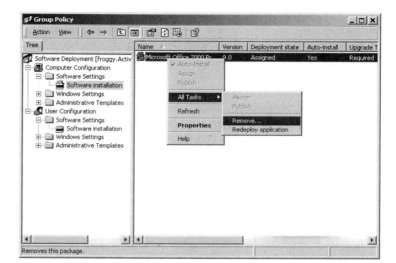

When choosing to remove a software package from a GPO, you have two options:

Immediately uninstall the software from users and computers.
You can choose this option so that an application is no longer available to users affected by the GPO. The program will be automatically uninstalled from users and/or computers that have the package.

Allow users to continue to use the software, but prevent new installations.   This option prevents users from making new installations of a package, but it does not remove the software if it has already been installed for users.

If you no longer require the ability to install or repair an application, you can delete it from your software distribution share point by deleting the appropriate Windows Installer package files. This will free up additional disk space for newer applications.

Optimizing and Troubleshooting Software Deployment

Although the features in Windows 2000 and the Active Directory make software deployment a relatively simple task, you should still consider many factors when making applications available on the network.

Here are some specific optimization and troubleshooting methods:

Test packages before deployment. Even though the Active Directory and GPOs make publishing and assigning applications easy, always test packages. The information gathered during these tests can be invaluable in helping the help desk and end users during a large-scale deployment.

Manage Group Policy scope and links. One of the most flexible aspects of deploying software with the Active Directory is the ability to assign Group Policy settings to users and computers. An easier way to manage multiple sets of applications may be to create separate GPOs for specific groups of applications. For example, one GPO could provide all end user productivity applications (such as Microsoft Office 2000 and Adobe Acrobat Reader) while another GPO could provide tools for users in the Engineering department.

Roll out software in stages. Installing software packages over the network can involve high bandwidth requirements and reduce the performance of production servers. Therefore, publish or assign applications to a few users at a time through GPOs and OUs.

Verify connectivity with the software distribution share. If clients can't communicate with the server that contains the software installation files, the installation will fail.

Organize categories. The list of applications available in a typical network environment can quickly grow very large. Organize programs based on functionality.

Create an installation log file. By using the `msiexec.exe` command, you can create an installation log file that records the actions attempted during the installation process and any errors generated.

Reduce redundancy.   Ensure that applications are not assigned or published to users through multiple GPOs. Though it may work, multiple GPOs can increase logon and GPO-processing time.

Manage software distribution points.   When users require applications, they will depend on the availability of installation shares. One method to guarantee greater performance and availability of these shares is to use the Windows 2000 Distributed File System (DFS). DFS allows for fault tolerance and the ability to use multiple servers to share commonly used files from a single logical share point, resulting in increased uptime, better performance, and easier access for end users.

Enforce consistency using MSI options.   One of the problems with applications and suites (such as Microsoft Office 2000) is that end users can decide which options are selected during installation. While it might be useful for some users, it can cause compatibility and management problems. Enforce standard configurations for applications.

Create Windows Installer files for older applications.   Although no tool included with Windows 2000 automatically performs this task, it is worth the time to create Windows Installer files for older applications. You may do so through third-party applications designed to monitor the Registry, file system, and changes an application makes during the setup process. The changes the application installation makes can be combined into a single MSI package for use in software deployment. This allows you to utilize the features of Windows Installer for applications that would not otherwise support it.

Necessary Procedures

Understanding the two necessary procedures for this objective—Creating a Software Deployment Share, and Publishing and Assigning Applications—can greatly ease network administration, besides make you more comfortable with the objective.

Creating a Software-Deployment Share

In this procedure you will prepare for software deployment by creating a directory share and placing certain types of files in this directory. In order to complete this procedure, you must have access to program installation files (via CD-ROM or through a network share) and 600MB of free disk space.

1. Using Windows Explorer, create a folder for use with application sharing. Be sure the volume on which you create this folder has at least 600MB of available disk space.

2. Within the folder, create another folder.

3. Copy the `adminpak.msi` file from the `%systemroot%\system32` folder to the subfolder you created in step 2.

4. Within the first folder, create another subfolder.

5. Copy all the installation files for a program of your choice from the CD-ROM or network share containing the files to the folder that you created in step 4.

6. Right-click the first folder (created in step 1) and select the Sharing tab. Choose Share This Folder and provide a share name of the folder created in step 1 and a comment of Software Distribution Share Point. Leave all other options as the default and click OK to create the share.

Publishing and Assigning Applications Using Group Policy

In this procedure you will create and assign applications to specific Active Directory objects using Group Policy Objects. In order to complete this procedure, you must have completed the first procedure, Creating a Software Deployment Share.

1. Open the Active Directory Users and Computers tool from the Administrative Tools program group.

2. Expand the domain and create a new top-level OU.

3. Within the OU create a user and login name. (Choose the defaults for all other options.)

4. Right-click the OU and select Properties.

5. Select the Group Policy tab, and click New. Type the name of a new GPO.

6. To edit the GPO, click Edit. Expand the Computer Configuration ➢ Software Settings object.

7. Right-click the Software Installation item and select New ➢ Package. Navigate to the share you created in the previous Necessary Procedure. Within the share double-click the folder created in step 4 of the previous procedure and select the installation file. Click Open.

8. In the Deploy Software dialog box, choose Advanced Published or Assigned and click OK. Note that the Published option is unavailable since applications cannot be published to computers.

9. To examine the Deployment options of this package, click the Deployment tab. Accept the default settings by clicking OK.

10. Within the Group Policy Editor, expand the User Configuration ➢ Software Settings object.

11. Right-click the Software Installation item and select New ➢ Package. Navigate to the share you created in the last Necessary Procedure. Within the share double-click the Admin Tools folder and select the `adminpak.msi` file. Click Open.

12. For the Software Deployment option, select Published and click OK.

13. Close the Group Policy Editor and then click Close to close the Properties of the Software OU.

Exam Essentials

Understand what Windows Installer does.   This system provides for better manageability of the software-installation process and gives you more control over the deployment process. Basically, it automates the installation of many of the programs you will use on the network.

Know what happens when you assign applications. When you assign an application to a user, the icons for the application appear in the Start menu, even though the application is not installed locally. Clicking on the icon for that application starts the installation process with Windows Installer. Applications assigned to the computer are visible to all users who are authenticated at that machine.

Understand what happens when you publish applications. Publishing differs from assigning. In publishing the users do not have icons. Rather, they can see the applications if they choose the Add/Remove Programs icon in Control Panel. By selecting an application, they can install it. Applications can only be published to users, not computers.

Key Terms and Concepts

Add/Remove Programs Icon in Control Panel that allows for the installation or removal of some applications.

application assignment scripts Store information regarding the assignment of programs and any settings made by the systems administrator.

assigning Assigning a software package makes the program available for automatic installation.

categories Groups of applications that share a similar scope or purpose.

initialization files Files that provide support for publishing non–Windows Installer applications.

patches Updates or fixes to released applications.

publishing Advertises the application to the user in the Add/Remove Programs portion of Control Panel, but does not provide the user with icons.

Transformation files Used for customizing the details of how applications are installed.

Windows Installer   Feature of Windows 2000 that allows for the automated installation of software programs across the network.

Windows Installer packages   Applications must include Windows Installer packages to be able to use Windows Installer.

Sample Questions

1. You want to ensure all users on your network will be able to run Microsoft Office 2000. Which of the following should you do?

   A. Publish the application to the computer.

   B. Publish the application to users.

   C. Assign the application to the computer.

   D. Assign the application to users.

   E. A or B

   F. C or D

   Answer: F. Assigning the application to users or computers will allow all users to have access to Microsoft Office 2000. All they need to do is click on the Office icon, and it will be installed if it is not already.

2. Which of the following operations does the Windows Installer support?

   A. Software deployment

   B. Software removal

   C. Software patches

   D. All of the above

   Answer: D. The Windows Installer supports all of the operations listed.

3. Which of the following Windows Installer settings prevents recovering from a failed installation?

A. Always Install with Elevated Privileges

B. Disable Rollback

C. Disable Search Order

D. Disallow Uninstall

E. None of the above

Answer: B. Disabling rollback can improve performance and reduce disk space requirements, but it prevents rolling back from a failed installation.

Deploy Windows 2000 by using Remote Installation Services (RIS).

One of the most painful parts of your job is likely to be associated with hardware and software rollouts. Deploying new computers begins with the installation of the operating system—a tedious task usually requiring you to sit in front of each new computer for at least an hour choosing appropriate options. The process may be repeated hundreds or even thousands of times, based on the size of the environment and the number of computers supported.

Not only can operating-system installation be boring, also it's difficult to remember all of the options that must be configured and to carry out the processes consistently on multiple installations. Clearly, you need a better solution.

Microsoft has included *Remote Installation Services (RIS)* components with Windows 2000 Server. RIS is designed to allow client computers to boot onto a network and immediately begin installing Windows 2000 Professional across the network.

Critical Information

The purpose of RIS is to minimize the problems and time associated with installing Windows 2000 Professional on computers. At the same time, it preserves the benefits of performing individual operating-system installations. RIS works through the creation of images and settings for a remote installation on a RIS server. Clients connect to the RIS server over the network and install the operating system using predefined settings.

One of the major benefits of RIS is that the hardware configuration does not have to be an exact match between client machines. The Windows 2000 Plug-and-Play and automatic-hardware-detection features will iron out any differences when the image is applied on client computers.

RIS works only with the Windows 2000 operating-system platform. Therefore, you must be running Windows 2000 Server (which acts as the RIS server), and you must plan to install Windows 2000 Professional on client computers.

RIS Server Requirements

RIS relies upon several different network and operating-system features to function properly. In order to take advantage of RIS, you must have the following services installed, configured, and enabled on your network:

- DNS (Domain Name System), used for resolving TCP/IP addresses to host names. Active Directory domain controllers and clients rely on DNS services for finding network resources.

- DHCP, (Dynamic Host Configuration Protocol), which automatically assigns TCP/IP configuration information to clients. DHCP is especially important for remote-boot clients, because they must be able to communicate on the network and connect to the RIS server.

- Active Directory, which hosts the Computer accounts used by RIS and allows you to control permissions to the domain. Also, the Active Directory's Group Policies are used to specify client options. (These services are required for use by RIS clients.) Finally, security permissions related to which users and computers can utilize remote installation are stored within the Active Directory.

When RIS is installed on a Windows 2000 Server computer, three services are automatically installed and configured:

Boot Information Negotiation Layer (BINL) The *Boot Information Negotiation Layer (BINL)* service checks that the correct computer is being installed and can be used to create a Computer account within an Active Directory domain.

Trivial File Transfer Protocol Daemon (TFTPD) When a client first connects to a RIS server computer, that client only has the bare minimum information required to communicate. At this stage, the *Trivial File Transfer Protocol Daemon (TFTPD)* service is used to transfer any required files from the server to the client.

Single Instance Store (SIS) *Single Instance Store (SIS)* technology is created to reduce the redundancy of data stored on a RIS server. If you were to create six images (with an average size of 300MB each), they would require 1.8GB of disk space. There is a lot of wasted space because most files between these images are the same. SIS is designed to eliminate this type of redundant storage by finding duplicate files and then replacing them with a link to one file.

Finally, you should be aware of the following minimum system requirements for a RIS server (as specified by Microsoft):

- Pentium-166 (or equivalent) processor
- 256MB RAM
- 2GB disk drive (reserved for use only by RIS)
- 10MB network adapter
- CD-ROM drive

The disk-space requirement is somewhat unique. The image files created for RIS must be stored on an NTFS volume that does not contain either the Windows 2000 system files or the boot files. The RIS process is resource intensive, especially with respect to disk input/output (I/O). Therefore, it is recommended that your RIS server computers exceed these values for better performance.

TIP   The volume you use to store RIS images should be used for nothing else.

RIS Client Requirements

On the client side, you must use a desktop computer with a network interface card or a laptop computer with a port replicator or docking station. Windows 2000 RIS does not support laptop or notebook computers that use PC Card or PCMCIA network adapters.

Client computers may use one of two methods to gain network access and connect to the RIS server:

Using a PXE Boot ROM   The *Preboot eXecution Environment (PXE)* specification is designed to allow computers with no operating system to access the network. The PXE Boot Read-Only Memory (ROM) chip is part of a computer's hardware, usually the network card. When the computer boots, it initializes the network adapter and then accesses the DHCP server to get a network address.

Using a Boot Floppy   Booting from a floppy is for computers without a PXE Boot ROM. You should boot from a floppy diskette containing the bare minimum information to connect to the network and communicate with the RIS server. Windows 2000 Server includes a utility to create these disks. In order to use a boot floppy for connecting to a RIS server, the client network adapter must be supported.

Client computers should meet the following minimum specifications:

- Pentium-166 (or equivalent) processor
- 32MB RAM

- 800MB hard disk

- Network adapter

- PXE Boot ROM version .99c or later

As with the server side, it is recommended that a computer have a faster processor, more memory, and a larger hard disk than the minimum. A faster network adapter also reduces the required installation time.

Installing RIS

Installation of RIS is a straightforward two-step procedure. First, you add the RIS service to a Windows 2000 Server and reboot the computer. Next, you configure the RIS server based on the options you require.

Configuring a RIS Server

Once RIS has been installed on the server, you need to configure the service to meet the needs of your network environment. Two main options can be configured for the RIS server:

Respond to all clients requesting service.   So enabled, the RIS server responds to remote-installation requests from clients. If this option is disabled, clients are not able to access the server for remote installation.

Do not respond to unknown client computers.   If this option is checked, a Computer object for the client requesting a remote installation must exist within the Active Directory domain. If a Computer account for the provided *Global Unique Identifier (GUID)* does not exist, the RIS server does not respond to the remote-installation request.

WARNING   You should choose RIS configuration options carefully because RIS in an unprotected network environment can be a security risk.

CREATING A CD-BASED IMAGE

A RIS server can contain one or more images of operating-system installation files. The images contain all the files necessary to install and configure the Windows 2000 Professional operating system via remote installation. You may create images two ways. The first involves creating a standard default image through the use of the Windows 2000 Professional CD-ROM. The second allows you to create custom images.

Once the Remote Installation Services Setup Wizard has completed, a new share is created on the server, called REMINST; it contains all files and settings to be used by clients to access the CD-based image.

CREATING A CUSTOM INSTALLATION

Although a CD-based image is sufficient for installing the base operating system, it does not allow you to add applications or make other changes to the configuration. The *Remote Installation Preparation Wizard (RIPrep)* utility is designed to do just that. The process for using RIPrep is as follows:

1. Install Windows 2000 Professional by using the CD-ROM or connecting to a network share that contains the necessary files.

2. Configure any operating-system settings you want to have copied to client computers. For example, you can change desktop settings to match your company's default settings. Or you may install optional Windows 2000 components such as Web services.

3. Install and configure any applications that should be installed as part of the image. This step is mainly used for older applications that do not use the new Microsoft Installer technology.

4. Close any open applications and then run the RIPrep utility. You will be asked to provide information about the RIS server to which this image will be saved, along with a title and description of the image. The RIPrep utility will collect information about operating-system settings and any applications installed on the system and then transmit the image to a RIS server.

After using the RIPrep utility, the RIS server will include a new custom image that can be used for installation. Figure 3.12 shows an example of the RIPrep utility.

FIGURE 3.12: Reviewing RIPrep installation settings

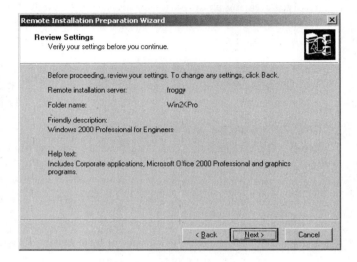

USING SETUP INFORMATION FILES (SIFS)

Windows 2000 Professional requires answers to many questions during the setup process. Although this can be done manually, it would be much better to preanswer the questions and store the settings in a file used by setup.

The specific installation options for the client are specified in a Setup Information File. These standard text files have the extension .SIF and can be edited to specify certain options to be used during installation. The following is a portion of the default ristndrd.sif file:

```
[data]
floppyless = "1"
msdosinitiated = "1"
OriSrc = "\\%SERVERNAME%\RemInst\
~CA%INSTALLPATH%\%MACHINETYPE%"
OriTyp = "4"
```

```
LocalSourceOnCD = 1

[SetupData]
OsLoadOptions = "/noguiboot /fastdetect"
SetupSourceDevice = "\Device\LanmanRedirector\
~CA%SERVERNAME%\RemInst\%INSTALLPATH%"

[Unattended]
OemPreinstall = no
NoWaitAfterTextMode = 0
FileSystem = LeaveAlone
ExtendOEMPartition = 0
ConfirmHardware = no
NtUpgrade = no
Win31Upgrade = no
TargetPath = \WINNT
OverwriteOemFilesOnUpgrade = no
OemSkipEula = yes
InstallFilesPath = "\\%SERVERNAME%\RemInst\
~CA%INSTALLPATH%\%MACHINETYPE%"

[UserData]
FullName = "%USERFULLNAME%"
OrgName = "%ORGNAME%"
ComputerName = %MACHINENAME%

[GuiUnattended]
OemSkipWelcome = 1
OemSkipRegional = 1
TimeZone = %TIMEZONE%
AdminPassword = "*"

[LicenseFilePrintData]
AutoMode = PerSeat

[Display]
```

```
ConfigureAtLogon = 0
BitsPerPel = 8
XResolution = 640
YResolution = 480
VRefresh = 60
AutoConfirm = 1

[Networking]
ProcessPageSections=Yes

[Identification]
JoinDomain = %MACHINEDOMAIN%
CreateComputerAccountInDomain = No
DoOldStyleDomainJoin = Yes

[NetProtocols]
MS_TCPIP=params.MS_TCPIP

[params.MS_TCPIP]
; transport: TC (TCP/IP Protocol)
InfID=MS_TCPIP
DHCP=Yes
```

If you have multiple images on your RIS server, you'll have multiple copies of the *.sif files. Each image uses its own Setup Information File, so you can use different sets of installation options. The *.sif file can be modified through any standard text editor (such as Windows Notepad).

Managing RIS Server Options

You can change the settings for a RIS server after it has been configured by opening the Active Directory Users and Computer tool, right-clicking the RIS Server object, and selecting Properties. On the Remote Install tab, you can change RIS options and settings.

By clicking the Show Clients button, you can automatically find any remote-installation clients on the network. Finding such clients is useful when you are determining which computers can be used with RIS.

You can also click the Advanced button to access more options for the RIS server. Here, you'll be able to set options for automatically determining the client computer name. The default options available include the following:

- First initial, last name

- Last name, first initial

- First name, last initial

- Last initial, first name

- Username

- NP Plus MAC (two standard characters followed by the Media Access Card address of the network adapter)

- Custom

For the Custom option, you can set several different options using variables (see Figure 3.13), which is extremely helpful if you are rolling out several computers and your organization already has a standard naming convention for client machines.

FIGURE 3.13: Setting default client-computer name settings

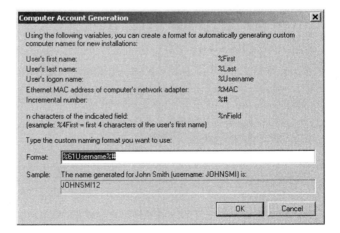

You can also set the location of the client account within the Active Directory. Options include:

Default Directory Service Location   Default Directory Service Location automatically saves the Computer object to the default location for clients, usually the Computers folder.

Same Location As That of the User Setting Up the Client Computer
Here, you save the Computer account in the Active Directory location in which the user performing the installation process resides. For example, if the user Jane Doe resides within the RIS OU, and this user performs the remote installation, then the Computer object will also reside within the RIS OU.

The Following Directory Service Location   Using this option allows you to specify a single Active Directory location for all new Computer objects.

By clicking the Images tab, you will be able to view a list of images available on a particular RIS server. You can also add new images, remove images (to make them unavailable for installation), and view the properties of an image (to see the title and description text).

By clicking the Add button, you will access a Wizard that allows you to generate either a new answer file (also known as a Setup Information File) or to generate a new installation image.

Setting Up a RIS Client

When performing an automated installation of Windows 2000 using RIS, you will normally be using a computer without an operating system. Therefore, the client must go through several steps before beginning the remote installation. The following process takes place when a RIS client computer is booted:

1. The computer gains network access through the use of a PXE Boot ROM or a RIS Boot floppy diskette.

2. The computer sends a broadcast over the network requesting an IP address; it also sends the computer's GUID.

3. A DHCP server on the network responds with a valid IP address.

4. The client initiates a remote-installation request.

5. The RIS server receives the request and looks in its database for the GUID of the client computer. If the GUID is found, it automatically begins the client installation. If the GUID is not found, the client is prompted to authenticate with the server using the Client Installation Wizard prompts.

6. Upon successful negotiation, the RIS server begins transferring files to the client, and the automated installation proceeds.

WARNING   During the client installation process, all information on the hard disk of the client will be lost. Be sure this is what you want before beginning the process.

Configuring Client-Setup Options

When the remote installation is started from the client, you may want to allow or disallow specific options. Four main options can be set for clients to choose during the RIS setup procedures:

Automatic Setup   When this option is chosen, you specify all of the installation options, and the user is not given any choices.

Custom Setup   Under Custom Setup, a user or systems administrator can stipulate various options, such as the name of the computer and the Active Directory location for the Computer object.

Restart Setup   In some cases the setup process may terminate before it is finished, due to a loss of network connectivity or a configuration problem. When the Restart Setup option is enabled, you may choose to restart setup from the point at which it failed.

Tools   When Tools is chosen, users or systems administrators can access various tools when the Client Installation Wizard is running.

For each of these settings, you can choose from among three policies: Allow, Don't Care, or Deny. Allow permits users or systems administrators to allow the particular setting during the client setup process, whereas Deny denies the privilege. Don't Care is the default setting, and it specifies no policy is set at that level. Settings at the parent or higher-level Active Directory objects may specify the Allow or Deny option.

Figure 3.14 shows where to find the options. You can access these settings by modifying the Group Policy Object for an Active Directory object and then clicking User Configuration ➤ Windows Settings ➤ Remote Installation Services.

FIGURE 3.14: Editing Group Policy settings for RIS

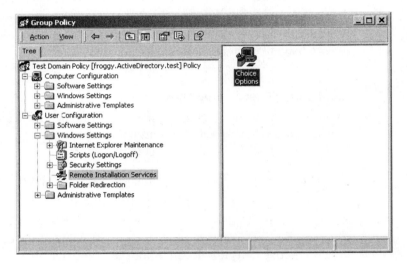

Using RIS through PXE-Compliant Network Adapters

In order to access the RIS server using the PXE-compliant network adapter, you must configure your computer to access the network during the boot process. This is done usually by accessing the system BIOS. The exact procedure should be available from the hardware manufacturer. Once connected to the RIS server, the rest of the installation process is the same as using a RIS boot disk.

Using RIS through a RIS Boot Disk

If your computer and network adapter do not support the PXE specification, you will need to create a boot disk, which can be created on a Windows 2000 server that has RIS installed. The purpose of the boot disk is the same as the purpose of the PXE Boot ROM—to load a minimal set of drivers to get the computer on the network. Once the computer has access to the network, the RIS server provides all required program code.

If your network adapter is not on the list during boot-disk creation, you will need to contact your computer manufacturer or network-card manufacturer in order to obtain the appropriate driver.

NOTE   Not all vendors will support remote-client installations using RIS.

If you have chosen the wrong network adapter for the boot disk, you will see the following message on the client computer when it boots:

```
Windows 2000 Remote Installation Boot Floppy

Error: Could not find a supported network card. The
boot floppy currently supports a limited set of PCI
based network cards for use with the Windows 2000
Remote Installation Service. Ensure this system
contains one of the supported network cards and try
the operation again. For assistance, contact your
systems administrator.
```

Performing the Client Installation

Once you have booted the client computer, either by a PXE device or a boot floppy, you will be connected to the RIS server. At this point, the text-mode portion of setup will begin. If you chose the Deny settings for all options, then the client will not be provided with any additional choices, and setup will automatically start copying files.

If, however, additional information is required (such as authentication information or a computer name), the Client Installation Wizard will appear. The Wizard will ask several questions to gather the required information. Once the information has been provided, the automated remote-installation process will begin.

Optimizing RIS Performance

The process of automatically installing an operating system can be bandwidth intensive. In the case of Windows 2000, the thousands of files required can lead to high network usage. If not managed properly, using RIS can reduce performance for all network users. Fortunately, there are several ways to optimize the performance of RIS in a network environment:

- Because of the high disk-I/O requirements for the automated client-installation process, it is usually a good idea to use a dedicated server for RIS operations.

- Using fast network links between RIS clients and servers can greatly increase performance. Even though it may be more expensive, the additional bandwidth will make the operation much faster. For the most part, trying to perform a RIS operation over a WAN link should be out of the question.

- By placing the RIS server and clients on the same dedicated subnet within your network, you can reduce the impact on performance that results from the load on routers. Additionally, by using a separate subnet, you reduce the chances of affecting other network users.

Troubleshooting RIS

Through the use of the configuration Wizards and Active Directory administration tools, it is usually a simple task to set up RIS the way you want it. In some instances, however, you may have problems in performing a remote installation.

If you're having trouble performing remote-installation options, there are several places to look:

Verify the server configuration.   Using the Active Directory Users and Computers tool, you can quickly and easily verify the proper functioning of a RIS server. To perform this test, open the Active Directory Users and Computers tool, right-click the name of the RIS server, and choose Properties. On the Remote Install tab, click the

Verify Server button. The Check Server Wizard will perform a diagnostic test on the current RIS configuration and then provide information on the configuration. If errors in the configuration are found, you should check the system event log for more information.

Verify the PXE Boot ROM version.   In order to be compatible with Windows 2000 Remote Installation Services, the PXE Boot ROM must be version .99c or greater. You may have problems booting and connecting to the RIS server if the client is using an earlier standard.

Verify the network-configuration settings.   Verify the network-configuration settings if the client is unable to connect to the RIS server. If the DHCP settings are incorrect, then the remote client may receive unusable TCP/IP address information. If other computers on the same network are using DHCP and are able to connect with the server, it's likely there is another problem.

Ensure that the RIS server contains the desired images.   Because there is no way for the client to specify which RIS server to connect to, the client may be connecting to the wrong RIS server on the network. This RIS server may not have all the images available on others.

Verify that you are using the correct boot disk.   The Windows 2000 Remote Boot disk contains network drivers for only one type of network-interface card. If you plan to install the Windows 2000 Professional operating system on multiple computers having different network adapters, you'll need to create multiple boot disks with different drivers.

Enable clients to choose options during the RIS setup process.   If the User Configuration Group Policy settings do not allow specific options, clients and systems administrators performing installations will be unable to change the settings. To change these settings, simply apply the appropriate Group Policy settings for the Computer object.

TIP   If you want to use multiple RIS servers (for performance and fault-tolerance reasons), ensure the appropriate images are available on all servers in your environment.

TIP RIS boot disks contain drivers for only one network card.

Necessary Procedures

The procedures for this objective walk you through the process of setting up RIS for client installations. First, you will install RIS and then configure it. Next, you will look at various RIS management options. Finally, you will create a RIS boot disk.

Installing Remote Installation Services

In this procedure you will install RIS. In order to complete this procedure, you must have access to the Windows 2000 Server CD-ROM or a network location that contains the necessary files.

1. Click Start ➤ Settings ➤ Control Panel. Double-click the Add/Remove Programs icon.

2. Click Add/Remove Windows Components.

3. To add a new item, click the Components button.

4. Place a check mark next to the Remote Installation Services item and then click Next.

5. If you have installed any optional Windows 2000 components that require additional configuration (such as Terminal Services), you will be prompted to enter configuration information for these items. The installation process will begin. When it has finished, you will be prompted to restart the computer. Choose Yes to restart the computer.

Configuring a CD-Based Image for RIS

In this procedure you will configure RIS to create a CD-based image of Windows 2000 Professional. In order to complete the steps in this procedure, you must first install RIS and have access to the Windows 2000 Professional installation files.

1. Click Start ➤ Settings ➤ Control Panel. Double-click the Add/ Remove Programs icon.

2. Click Add/Remove Windows Components. Highlight the Configure Remote Installation Services item and then click the Configure button.

3. You will see the introductory information for the Remote Installation Services Setup Wizard. Click Next to continue.

4. Specify the folder to which the remote-installation information will be written. Select a path on a local physical drive formatted as an NTFS v5 partition that is neither the boot nor system partition. Ensure that this partition has at least 400MB free (although you will need more if you plan to store many different images). Click Next.

5. On the Initial Settings step, place a check mark next to the Respond to Client Computers Requesting Service option to enable RIS for use by clients. Click Next.

6. Specify the source-file location for the Windows installation files. Insert the Windows 2000 Professional CD-ROM and enter the path to this drive. Alternatively, you can browse for the installation files (which may be on the local system or located on a network drive) by clicking Browse. Once you have selected the appropriate path, click Next to continue.

7. Specify the name of the folder to which the installation files will be copied. The default location will be titled win2000.pro. If you are using multiple images, it is a good idea to use a clear, descriptive name for the image file. Click Next to continue.

8. Specify a friendly name and a description for this RIS image. This information will be visible by users and systems administrators performing remote installations. Therefore, you should make the description as meaningful as possible. Click Next to continue.

9. Finally, you are given an opportunity to review the settings. Check that the correct paths have been provided. To complete the installation, click Finish.

10. The RIS Wizard will begin copying the necessary files to the location you specified. This process is likely to take several minutes. Once finished, you will see a summary of the steps performed. To complete the operation, click Done.

11. Close the Add/Remove Programs dialog box and the Control Panel.

Managing RIS Server Options

In this procedure you will view the various options available when configuring a RIS server. In order to perform this procedure, you must have first installed RIS on the local computer.

1. Open the Active Directory Users and Computers tool.

2. Find the local domain controller within the Active Directory structure. Right-click the name of this computer and select Properties.

3. Select the Remote Install tab. Note that you have the option to verify the configuration of the current server. To see any clients able to use this RIS server, click Show Clients.

4. Click Advanced Settings to view additional options for the RIS server.

5. On the New Clients tab, select Username for the Generate Client Computer Names Using selection. To see other options, click Customize. Click OK.

6. To manage images, click the Images tab. Note that the list includes any images already available for installation. You can find additional information about the images by clicking Properties.

7. Finally, click the Tools tab. By default, this tab will be blank. If, however, you installed additional Microsoft or third-party tools related to RIS, they will show up here.

8. Click OK twice to close the settings for the RIS server.

9. When finished, close the Active Directory Users and Computers tool.

Creating a Remote Boot Disk

This procedure has you create a remote-boot disk. In order to complete this procedure, you must have first installed and configured RIS. You will also need a single, high-density floppy diskette.

1. Using Windows Explorer, open the folder into which you placed the Remote Installation files.

2. Within this folder open the Admin\i386 folder.

3. To open the Windows 2000 Remote Boot Disk Generator, double-click the `rbfg` program.

4. To specify the network adapter of the client computer, click the Adapter List button. Select the appropriate network adapter from the list. Click OK.

5. To create the boot diskette, click Create Disk. The Windows 2000 Remote Boot Disk Generator will begin copying the necessary file(s) to the floppy.

6. When finished, click Close to exit the Windows 2000 Remote Boot Disk Generator.

Exam Essentials

Understand the scope of RIS.   RIS can only be used in a Windows 2000 environment for installing Windows 2000 Professional clients.

Understand the requirements for using RIS.   DNS, DHCP, and Active Directory must all be running to use RIS.

Know how to connect clients to a RIS server.   Clients can connect either using PXE boot ROM or by using a RIS boot disk.

Know how to create RIS images, including custom images.   In order to create RIS images, you need access to the Windows 2000 installation files. These can either be on CD or on a network share. The Remote Installation Preparation Wizard (RIPrep) utility is designed to set up custom images.

Key Terms and Concepts

Boot Information Negotiation Layer (BINL)   Service responsible for determining that the correct computer is being installed and can be used to create a Computer account within an Active Directory domain.

Global Unique Identifier (GUID)   Number that uniquely identifies the client computer on the network.

Preboot eXecution Environment (PXE)   Specification designed to allow computers with no operating system to access the network.

Remote Installation Services (RIS)   Windows 2000 service designed to alleviate the problems and minimize the time associated with installing Windows 2000 Professional on computers.

Remote Installation Preparation Wizard (RIPrep)   Utility designed to create custom RIS images.

Single Instance Store (SIS)   Method used to reduce the redundancy of data stored on a RIS server.

Trivial File Transfer Protocol Daemon (TFTPD)   Service used to transfer required files from the server to the client.

Sample Questions

1. The RIS root directory can be which of the following?

   A. The boot partition

   B. The system partition

   C. A FAT partition

   D. A FAT32 partition

   E. None of the above

   Answer: E. The RIS root directory must reside on a partition that is formatted using the NTFS file system and is not a system or boot partition.

2. Windows 2000 Remote Installation Services (RIS) can be used to install which of the following operating systems?

   A. Windows NT 4 Workstation

   B. Windows 2000 Professional

   C. Windows 2000 Server

   D. Windows 2000 Advanced Server

   E. All of the above

   Answer: B. RIS supports only the automated installation of Windows 2000 Professional.

3. You want to make some changes to the default setup for an existing image. Which file or object should you modify?

   A. OU Properties

   B. Group Policy Objects (GPOs)

   C. Domain policy

   D. Setup Information Files (*.sif)

   E. None of the above

   Answer: D. Setup Information Files specify the basic options used during automated installation.

Configure RIS security.

Remote Installation Services allows you to easily install a standard Windows 2000 Professional workstation on your network. However, unauthorized use of RIS can lead to security breaches. It's important not only to know how to set up and use RIS, but also to protect the network from violations.

Critical Information

Before you install a remote-client computer, you should first create a computer account within the domain, to be used during installation. When you create the computer account, you will need to set sufficient permissions to allow users to modify it during installation.

Although you may allow remote clients to request a remote installation from the RIS server, this option reduces security because any valid domain account with appropriate permissions will be able to install the image to a client computer. Furthermore, you wouldn't be able to control to *which* computer the image will be applied.

Another problem arises when multiple RIS servers exist in the same network environment. It would thus be difficult to tell which RIS server responded to the client first and whether it contains the correct images.

Prestaging Client Computers

How can systems administrators control the machines that will receive remote-installation images? The main method is by *prestaging* client computer accounts within the Active Directory. Prestaging involves the creation of a client account, supplying a GUID for the computer, and specifying the RIS server(s) from which the remote installation can be requested.

In order for computers on the network to be uniquely identified, some number or value must be dedicated to each machine. For computers that have them, the GUID or *Universally Unique Identifier (UUID)* can be used. These values are set by computer manufacturers and reside in the computers' BIOS.

The format of the 32-digit, hexadecimal GUID number is eight digits, followed by three sets of four digits, followed by 12 digits. For example, the following is a valid GUID:

```
01234567-ABCD-1234-ABCD-01234567890AB
```

RIS servers can be configured to respond to specific machine addresses. This adds security to a network environment, as it prevents any user from adding a computer to the network and joining the Active Directory. Although it is recommended that this type of security be enabled, the RIS server may also be configured to allow connections from any computer on the network. When this option is chosen, a systems administrator is not required to enter in a GUID when the computer account is created.

Delegating Permissions to Create Computer Accounts

In addition to setting permissions on specific computer accounts, you can use the Delegation of Control Wizard to allow specific users to create accounts within the domain.

The Delegation of Control Wizard within the Active Directory Users and Computers tool is used to assign the appropriate permissions. In the Active Directory Users and Computers tool, right-click the domain name and select Properties. Select Delegate Control. The Wizard will walk you through the steps required to select users and/ or groups. As shown in Figure 3.15, you must select the Join a Computer to the Domain permission.

FIGURE 3.15: Delegating control to join a computer to the domain

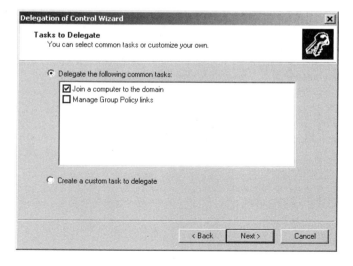

Once you have allowed certain users the permissions to add a computer to the domain, you will not be required to create Computer objects before starting the installation process. Of course, in order for the added computers to have access to the RIS server, you must not have stipulated that computer accounts exist within the domain before the process begins.

In order to allow the creation of Computer objects within an OU, you will need to modify any Group Policy Objects that apply to the OU. The specific setting to modify can be found in Computer Configuration ➤ Windows Settings ➤ Security Settings ➤ Local Policies ➤ User Rights Assignment. As shown in Figure 3.16, you can add the User and Group objects that will enable you to add computers to the domain by modifying the Add Workstations to Domain option.

FIGURE 3.16: Setting User Rights to add a computer to the domain

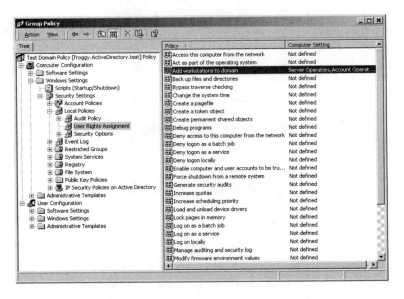

Authorizing a RIS Server

Before a RIS server is made available to clients, a systems administrator must authorize it. Requiring authorization of a server adds a measure of security by preventing other individuals from adding new RIS servers to the network.

Necessary Procedures

For thorough understanding of this objective, you should practice creating computer accounts and authorizing RIS servers.

Creating a Computer Account

In this procedure you will create a Computer object within the Active Directory and add the necessary permissions for a user to add the client computer to the Active Directory domain.

1. Open the Active Directory Users and Computers tool.

2. Create a top-level OU.

3. Within the OU, create a new User object with a name and logon name (choose the defaults for all other options).

4. Within the OU, create a Computer object. Click the Change button to specify the users and groups that will be able to add this computer to a domain. Select the new user from the list of users and click OK. Click Next.

5. In the Managed dialog box, place a check mark next to the This Is a Managed Computer option. Enter the GUID/UUID value, including brackets, like in the following example:

```
{123FB937-ED12-11BD-BACD-076A01878937}
```

6. Click Next. For the Host Server selection, select the Any Available Remote Installation Server option and then click Next. Note that you could choose servers from within a specific Active Directory domain if you have multiple RIS servers on the network or if you want the RIS process to be restricted to only one machine.

7. Click Finish to create the computer account.

8. When finished, close the Active Directory Users and Computers tool.

Authorizing a RIS Server

In this procedure you will authorize a DHCP server and a RIS server. In order to complete the steps in this exercise, you must have installed and configured RIS, but not yet authorized either DHCP or RIS.

1. Log in to the computer as a member of the Domain Admins or Enterprise Admins group.

2. Open the DHCP snap-in from the Administrative Tools program group.

3. Right-click the name of the local computer and click Authorize.

4. When you are finished authorizing the server, close the DHCP administrative tool.

Exam Essentials

Understand what prestaging a computer account means.   Prestaging means the computer is given permission to be installed on the network before the installation begins. The computer identifies itself to the RIS server via a unique number, either a GUID or UUID.

Key Terms and Concepts

prestaging   Setting up computer accounts in the domain for clients by using their GUID or UUID numbers.

Universally Unique Identifier (UUID)   Number that uniquely identifies a particular machine on the network.

Sample Questions

1. Hardware-based Global Unique Identifiers (GUIDs) are used to uniquely identify computers. They are assigned by hardware manufacturers and are hard-coded into which of the following areas of a computer?

A. The hard disk

B. The smart card

C. The BIOS

D. None of the above

Answer: C. GUIDs are used to uniquely identify computers in a networked environment and are assigned by computer manufacturers, hard-coded into BIOS.

2. Which of the following is/are true regarding prestaging of RIS clients? (Assume there is only one RIS server on the network.)

A. Prestaging increases performance.

B. Prestaging decreases performance.

C. Prestaging increases security.

D. Prestaging decreases security.

E. Both A and C

Answer: C. Prestaging increases security by specifying that only certain computers can perform a remote installation from a RIS server.

Chapter

4

Managing, Monitoring, and Optimizing the Components of Active Directory

---

MICROSOFT EXAM OBJECTIVES COVERED IN THIS CHAPTER:

Manage Active Directory objects. *(pages 178 – 199)*

- Move Active Directory objects.

- Publish resources in Active Directory.

- Locate objects in Active Directory.

- Create and manage accounts manually or by scripting.

- Control access to Active Directory objects.

Manage Active Directory performance. *(pages 199 – 223)*

- Monitor, maintain, and troubleshoot domain controller performance.

- Monitor, maintain, and troubleshoot Active Directory components.

Manage and troubleshoot Active Directory replication. *(pages 223 – 228)*

- Manage intersite replication.

- Manage intrasite replication.

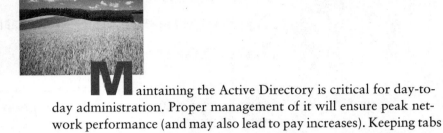

aintaining the Active Directory is critical for day-to-day administration. Proper management of it will ensure peak network performance (and may also lead to pay increases). Keeping tabs on performance, especially on critical servers, can head off many potential costly problems.

An important aspect of managing is keeping objects up-to-date. If users transfer departments, the network should reflect that change. If sales and marketing join forces, their network objects should follow suit. Delegating such mundane administration responsibilities, while keeping the network secure, can free you up for more daunting challenges.

Allowing all users to easily access needed information, regardless of the users' physical location, will keep the powers-that-be happy. Site replication facilitates easy information access and can be performed within one site, as well as between sites.

▶ Manage Active Directory objects.

The main tool to manage the objects within the Active Directory is the *Active Directory Users and Computers tool*. Using this Microsoft Management Console (MMC) snap-in, you will be able to create, manage, and control Active Directory objects.

You know how hierarchical structures can be created within domains using OUs. These structures are designed to map to the administrative and physical layouts of your network. Stopping the hierarchy at the OU level does a disservice to the Active Directory. The real purpose of the Active Directory is managing objects.

Critical Information

Several different types of Active Directory objects can be created and managed. The objects represent the various items in your network environment:

Computer   *Computer objects* are used for managing workstations in the environment.

Contact   Contacts are not security principals like Users, but are used for specifying information about individuals within the organization. *Contact objects* are usually used in OUs to designate the main administrative contact.

Group   Groups are security principals. That is, they are created for assigning and managing permissions. Groups contain user accounts.

Organizational Unit   An organizational unit (OU) is created to build a hierarchy within the Active Directory domain. It is the smallest unit used to create administrative groupings and can be used for assigning Group Policies. Generally, the OU structure within a domain will reflect a company's business organization.

Printer   *Printer objects* map to printers.

Shared Folder   *Shared Folder objects* map to server shares and are used for organizing the various file resources that may be available on file/print servers.

User   A *user object* is the fundamental security principal on which the Active Directory is based. User accounts contain information about individuals, as well as password and other permission information.

By default, after you install and configure a domain controller, you will see the following sections of organization within the Active Directory Users and Computers tool:

Built-In   The *Built-In container* includes all standard groups installed by default when you promote a domain controller. These groups are used for administering the servers in your environment, such as the Administrators group, Backup Operators, and Print Operators.

Computers By default, the *Computers container* contains a list of the workstations in your domain.

Domain Controllers The *Domain Controllers container* includes a list of all of the domain controllers for the domain.

Foreign Security Principals *Security principals* are Active Directory objects to which permissions can be applied. *Foreign security principals* are any objects not part of the current domain, but to which security can be assigned.

Users The *Users container* includes all security accounts of the domain. When you first install the domain controller, several groups will dwell in this container. For example, the Domain Admins group and the Administrator account are created in this container.

Managing Active Directory Objects

Once the necessary Active Directory objects have been created, you'll probably need to make changes to their default properties. Active Directory allows you to modify several properties for each object.

NOTE For specific procedures involving creation of Active Directory objects, please see *Windows 2000 Directory Services Administration Study Guide.*

Many common options exist for Active Directory objects. For example, Groups and Computers both have a Managed By tab.

TIP Familiarize yourself with the different options available for different objects.

Filtering and Advanced Options

The Active Directory Users and Computers tool has a couple other features that come in quite handy when managing many objects. You can access one by clicking the View menu in the MMC console and choosing Filter Options. You'll see a dialog box similar to the one shown in Figure 4.1. Here, you can choose to filter objects by type. Additionally, you can create more complex filters by choosing Create Custom Filter. Under this option you will see an interface similar to the Find interface.

FIGURE 4.1: Filtering objects using the Active Directory Users and Computers tool

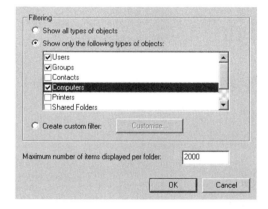

Another feature in the Active Directory Users and Computers tool is Advanced options, enabled by clicking Advanced Options in the View menu. Enabling Advanced options will add two top-level folders to the list under the name of the domain. The System folder (shown in Figure 4.2) lists additional features that can be configured to work with the Active Directory, such as Distributed File System (DFS), IP Security policies, and the File Replication Service. In addition to the System folder, you'll also see the *LostAndFound* folder, which contains any files not replicated properly between domain controllers.

TIP Check the LostAndFound folder periodically for files, so you can move them or copy them to other locations, if necessary.

FIGURE 4.2: Advanced options in the Active Directory Users and Computers tool

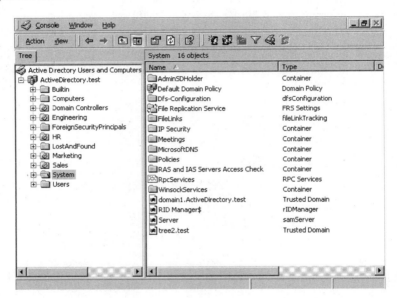

Moving, Renaming, and Deleting Objects

Moving objects—which is useful if objects have been created in the wrong OU or if a user switches departments or locations—is done through the Active Directory Users and Computers tool. You can also easily rename objects here, by right-clicking an object and selecting Rename. Note that this option does not apply to all objects. For example, in order to prevent security breaches, computer objects cannot be renamed. Additionally, you can remove objects from the Active Directory by right-clicking them and choosing Delete.

WARNING   Deleting an Active Directory object is an irreversible action. When an object is destroyed, any security permissions or other settings made for that object are removed as well. Because each object within the Active Directory contains its own security identifier (SID), simply re-creating an object with the same name will not generate the same SID; therefore, the previous permissions associated with it will be gone.

Publishing Active Directory Objects

An important aspect of managing Active Directory objects is controlling which objects users can see. The act of making an Active Directory object available is known as *publishing*. The two main publishable objects are Printers and Shared Folders.

The general process for creating server shares and shared printers remains unchanged from previous versions of Windows. You still need to create the various objects (a printer or a file-system folder) and then enable the objects for sharing. To make the resources available via the Active Directory, the resources must also be published there.

You can also publish Windows NT 4 resources through the Active Directory by creating Active Directory objects for those resources.

TIP   When publishing objects in the Active Directory, you should know the server name and share name of the resource.

You can change the resource to which the Active Directory objects point without having to reconfigure or even notify clients. For example, if you move a share from one server to another, you need only update the shared folder properties to point to the new location. Active Directory clients will still refer to the resource with the same path and name as before.

Without the Active Directory, Windows NT 4 shares and printers will only be accessible through the use of NetBIOS. If you're planning to disable the NetBIOS protocol in your environment, you must be sure these resources have been published, or they will not be accessible.

Publishing Printers and Shared Folders

Printers can be easily published within the Active Directory. Note that when you create and share a printer, an Active Directory Printer object is not displayed within the Active Directory Users and Computers tool. The printer is actually associated with the computer object to which it is shared.

Once you have created and published the shared folder, clients can use the My Network Places icon to find the Printer object. The shared folder will be organized based on the OU in which you created the Shared Folder object.

TIP Though beyond the scope of this book, the Windows 2000 Distributed File System (DFS) service allows for the use of hierarchical shares. The Active Directory Shared Folders object is completely compatible with this method.

Once created, you will likely want to restrict resources' use to certain clients and groups. In addition to setting permissions for end users, you can also use the Delegation of Control Wizard to assign management permissions to objects.

Searching the Active Directory

All your resource information is located in the Active Directory, and, through the Find feature of the Active Directory Users and Computers tool, you should be able to easily find any object you're looking for. The more information you enter in for each object, the easier objects are to find.

Implementing Active Directory Security

Within the Administrative Tools folder on domain controllers, you will find three useful tools for setting and managing Active Directory and domain controller security:

Local Security Policy   The settings here pertain to the local computer only; they are useful when you have specific computers that require custom security configurations. For example, an intranet Web server may have different settings from a mission-critical database server.

Domain Security Policy   The *Domain Security Policy* utility is used to view security settings that apply to all objects within a domain. Using this utility, you can specify settings such as the audit policy and System Service settings. The Domain Security Policy settings will apply to all domain controllers within a domain, unless they are specifically overridden.

Domain Controller Security Policy   The options presented within the *Domain Controller Security Policy* are similar to those found in the Domain Security Policy utility. The major difference is the settings you make with this tool apply only to the local domain controller rather than to all domain controllers within the domain.

You can add Users to Groups regardless of the OU in which they're contained. This flexibility allows you to easily manage user and group accounts based on your business organization.

The Active Directory Users and Computers tool also lets you perform common functions by simply right-clicking an object and selecting actions from the context-sensitive menu.

Delegating Control of Active Directory Objects

You can use OUs to logically group, and therefore easily manage, objects. Once you have placed the appropriate Active Directory objects within OUs, you will be ready to delegate control of these objects.

Creating Accounts through Scripting

Although the Active Directory Users and Computers tool provides an intuitive way to create and manage objects, sometimes it is not the best solution. Imagine creating several hundred user accounts. Clearly, using the point-and-click interface is inefficient. This is especially true if the information already exists in another format—such as a text file or an Excel spreadsheet.

Through scripting and import/export processes, you can make such a task much more manageable. The focus here will be on an overview of methods. You'll likely need to consult other resources to carry out customizations for your own environment.

CSVDE

The *Comma-Separated Value Directory Exchange (CSVDE)* tool enables you to import and export Active Directory information from and to comma-separated value (CSV) text files. CSV files are commonly used to transfer information between different types of data-storage systems. If you wanted to transfer information between a mainframe application and an Excel spreadsheet, you could use a CSV text file as an intermediate, since both applications read this format.

Another useful feature of CSV files is they can be easily edited with any standard text editor or applications that support this format. The CSVDE utility is run from the command line.

NOTE For specific options of the CSVDE utility, read *Windows 2000 Directory Services Administration Study Guide.*

Before importing new user accounts, always perform an export first so you can view the structure of the file and the information you'll need. You can then make changes to this file and import it later.

You can greatly simplify the import process if you use an application that can read and properly format CSV files. Microsoft Excel is a good example. You can also cut and paste values from other Microsoft Excel spreadsheets into the same import file.

LDIFDE

The main method to query the Active Directory is through the *Lightweight Directory Access Protocol* (LDAP). LDAP is commonly used for querying many directory sources, such as X.500-based directories and Novell Directory Services (NDS). The *LDAP Interchange Format* (LDIF) provides a common data-storage and transfer mechanism for working with LDAP-based data. LDIF files can contain the instructions required to create, modify, and delete objects.

The *LDIF Directory Exchange* (LDIFDE) command is similar to the CSVDE command, except the intermediate file is in the LDIF format. Of course, you would only want to use LDIF for applications that support this format. It is not designed for use with Microsoft Excel or Notepad, for example.

Windows Script Host (WSH)

Although the LDIFDE and CSVDE utilities provide a good way to import and export data, sometimes you need to perform more complicated modifications to data. Suppose you wanted to programmatically change all of your usernames to conform to your company's new naming convention. These types of actions are best performed through scripting methods.

The *Windows Script Host* (WSH) environment was designed to allow you to quickly and easily create simple files that automate common functions. Among the various functions that can be performed by WSH are:

- Creating Active Directory objects, including users, groups, and printers

- Modifying or deleting Active Directory objects

- Performing network logon functions, such as mapping network drives

- Starting and stopping services

- Accessing Microsoft Office or other applications and performing common tasks

WSH is actually a scripting host, as opposed to a programming language. Therefore, it allows for the use of many different languages. Specifically, WSH ships with support for VBScript and JScript. Additionally, third-party developers can write interpreters for PERL and other types of scripts.

Two main executables are used to launch files that are compatible with WSH:

- Cscript, the command-line version of the scripting host

- Wscript, the Windows GUI version of the scripting host

For more information on obtaining and using WSH, see `http://msdn.microsoft.com/scripting/`. This site includes the entire object model for WSH, sample script files, tutorials, and VBScript/JScript language references.

Necessary Procedures

You will review several necessary procedures for this objective. Being able to create, manage, and secure objects within Active Directory is essential to understanding Windows 2000.

Creating Active Directory Objects

In this procedure you will create some basic Active Directory objects. You must have first installed and configured at least one Active Directory domain. This procedure is necessary to complete later procedures.

1. Open the Active Directory Users and Computers tool.

2. Expand the current domain to list the objects currently contained within it. You should see folders.

3. Create a new top-level OU by right-clicking the name of the domain and selecting New ➤ Organizational Unit. When prompted for the name of the OU, type one and click OK.

4. Repeat step 3 to create more top-level OUs.

5. Right-click the OU created in step 3 and select New ➢ User. Fill in the information. Click Next to continue.

6. Enter in a password for this user and then confirm it. Note that you can also make changes to password settings here. Click Next. You will see a summary of the user information. Click OK to create the new user.

7. Create another user in one of the containers created in step 4. Click Next to continue. Assign a password. Click Next and then click Finish to create the user.

8. Right-click the OU and select New ➢ Shared Folder. Enter a name and network path. Note that if the resource does not exist, the object can still be created. Click OK to create the Shared Folder object.

9. Right-click another OU created in step 4 and select New ➢ Group. Type **All Users** for the group name (for pre–Windows 2000, leave the Group Name field with the same value). For the Group Scope, select Global, and for the Group type, select Security. To create the group, click OK.

10. Right-click another OU created in step 4 and select New ➢ Computer. Type the name of the computer. Notice that the pre–Windows 2000 name will automatically be populated and that, by default, the members of the Domain Admins group will be the only ones able to add this computer to the domain. Place a check mark in the Allow Pre–Windows 2000 Computers to Use This Account box and then click OK to create the Computer object.

11. Close the Active Directory Users and Computers tool.

Managing Object Properties

In this procedure you will modify the properties for Active Directory objects. In order to complete the steps in this procedure, you must have completed the first procedure.

1. Open the Active Directory Users and Computers tool.

2. Expand the name of the domain and select an OU. Right-click an account and select Properties.

3. Here, you will see the various Properties tabs for the User account. The basic tabs include the following:

General: General account information about this user

Address: The physical location information about this user

Account: User logon name and other account restrictions such as workstation restrictions and logon hours

Profile: Information about the user's roaming profile settings

Telephones: Telephone contact information for the user

Organization: The user's title, department, and company information

Member Of: Group membership information for the user

Dial-In: Remote Access Service (RAS) permissions for the user

Environment: Logon and other network settings for the user

Sessions: Session limits, including maximum session time and idle session settings

Remote Control: Sets remote-control options for this user's session

Terminal Services Profile: Sets information about the user's profile for use with Windows 2000 Terminal Services

Click OK to continue.

4. Select another OU. Right-click the All Users Group and click Properties. In the dialog box, you will be able to modify the membership of the group. Click the Members tab and then click Add. Add accounts to the Group. Click OK to save the settings and then OK to accept the group modifications.

5. Select still another OU. Right-click a Computer object. Notice that you can choose to disable the account or reset it (to allow another computer to join the domain under the same name). From the right-click menu, choose Properties. You'll see the properties for the Computer object. The various tabs in this dialog include the following:

General: Information about the name of the computer, the role of the computer, and its description. Note that you can allow the Local System Account of this machine to request services from other servers—useful if the machine is a trusted and secure computer.

Operating System: The name, version, and service-pack information for the operating system running on the computer.

Member Of: The Active Directory groups of which the Computer object is a member.

Location: A description of where the computer is physically located.

Managed By: Information about the user or contact object responsible for managing the computer.

After you have examined the available options, click OK to continue.

6. Select an OU. Right-click a user account, and choose Reset Password. You will be prompted to enter a new password and then asked to confirm it. Note that you can also force the user to change this password upon the next logon.

7. Close the Active Directory Users and Computers tool.

Moving Active Directory Objects

In this procedure you will make several changes to the organization of Active Directory objects. In order to complete this procedure, you must have completed the first procedure for this objective.

1. Open the Active Directory Users and Computers tool and expand the name of the domain.

2. Select an OU, right-click a Computer object, and select Move. A dialog box will appear. Select a second OU and click OK to move the Computer object to that container.

3. Click the second OU and verify that the Computer object was moved.

4. Close the Active Directory Users and Computers tool.

Creating and Publishing a Printer

In this procedure you will create and share a printer. In order to complete the installation of the printer, you will require access to the Windows 2000 installation media (via the hard disk, a network share, or the CD-ROM drive).

1. Click Start ➤ Settings ➤ Printers. Double-click Add New Printer. This will start the Add Printer Wizard. Click Next to begin.

2. In the Network or Local Printer box, select Local Printer. Uncheck the Automatically Detect and Install My Plug and Play Printer box. Click Next.

3. In the Select the Printer Port dialog box, select Use the Following Port. From the list below that option, select LPT1: Printer Port. Click Next.

4. Select the manufacturer. Click Next.

5. When asked for the name of the printer, type it. Click Next.

6. When prompted for the share name, select Share As and type a name. Click Next.

7. Fill in the location. Click Next.

8. When prompted to print a test page, select No. Click Next.

9. You will see a confirmation of the printer options you selected. Click Finish to create the printer.

10. You will now need to verify that the printer will be listed in the Active Directory. In the Printers folder, right-click the printer icon and select Properties. Next, select the Sharing tab and ensure that the List in the Directory box is checked. Note that you can also add

additional printer drivers for other operating systems using this tab. Click OK to accept the settings. Close the Printers window.

11. Now that the printer has been created and shared, you need to verify that it is available for use. Click Start ➤ Search ➤ For Printers. In order to search for all printers, leave all of the options blank. Note that you can use the Features and Advanced tabs to restrict the list of printers to those that match certain requirements. Click Find Now. You should receive results that demonstrate the printer is available through the Active Directory.

12. When finished, exit the Find dialog box.

Creating and Publishing a Shared Folder

In this procedure you will create and publish a shared folder. It is assumed you will be using the C: partition; however, you may want to change the partition based on your server configuration. You must have completed the first procedure for this objective.

1. Create a new folder in the root directory of your C: partition and name it.

2. Right-click the folder and select Sharing.

3. On the Sharing tab, select Share This Folder. For the Share Name, type one in. Leave the user limit, permissions, and caching settings as their defaults. Click OK to create the share.

4. To verify the share has been created, click Start ➤ Run and type the UNC path for the local server. For instance, if the server were named DC1, you would type \\dc1. The path will connect you to the local computer where you can view any available network resources. Verify that the folder exists and then close the window.

5. Open the Active Directory Users and Computers tool. Expand the current domain and right-click an OU. Select New ➤ Shared Folder.

6. In the dialog box, type the name of the folder. Then, type the UNC path to the share (for example, \\DC1\Test Share). Click OK to create the share.

7. Now that you have created the shared folder in the Active Directory, it's time to verify it. Right-click the name of the domain and select Find.

8. On the Find menu, select Shared Folders. Leave the remaining options blank to search for all Active Directory shares. (Notice that you can also use the Advanced tab to further specify information about the share you are searching for.) Click the Find Now button to obtain the results of the search.

9. Close the Find dialog box and exit the Active Directory Users and Computers tool.

Finding Objects in the Active Directory

In this procedure you will search for specific objects in the Active Directory. In order to complete this procedure, you must have completed the first procedure for this objective.

1. Open the Active Directory Users and Computers tool.

2. Right-click the name of the domain and select Find.

3. In the Find field, select Users, Computers, and Groups. For the In setting, choose Entire Directory to search the entire Active Directory environment for the criteria you enter. Note that if this is a production domain and if there are many objects, this may be a time-consuming and network-intensive operation.

4. In the Name field, type a valid name and then click Find Now to obtain the results of the search.

5. You should have found several results. To narrow the list, click the Advanced tab. In the Fields drop-down list, select User ➢ Last Name. For the Condition, select Starts With, and for the Value, type a last name. Click Add to add this item to the search criteria. Click Find Now. Notice that this time, only the user and contact that have the last name are shown.

6. To filter the result set even further, click the View menu and select Filter. The filter is displayed in the row just above the Results windows. In the Name field, type the user's first name and press Enter. The result is filtered to the user's first name.

7. To view more information about the user object, you can right-click it and select Properties.

8. To quickly view (and filter) more information about multiple objects, select the View menu and choose Select Columns. By selecting fields and clicking Add, you will be able to view more information about the retrieved objects. Click OK to add the information.

9. When you are finished searching, close the Find box and exit the Active Directory Users and Computers tool.

Delegating Control of Active Directory Objects

In this procedure you will delegate control of Active Directory objects. In order to complete the steps in this procedure, you must first create the OUs and objects necessary.

1. Open the Active Directory Users and Computers tool.

2. Create a new user within an OU, filling in the first and last names and the logon name. Use the default settings for other fields.

3. Right-click a second OU and select Delegate Control. The Delegation of Control Wizard will now start. Click Next.

4. To add users and groups to which you want to delegate control, click Add. From the list of users, select the user you created in step 2. Click OK and then Next to continue.

5. Select the Delegate the Following Common Tasks option and place a check mark next to the following options:

> Create, Delete, and Manage User Accounts
>
> Reset Passwords on User Accounts
>
> Read All User Information
>
> Create, Delete, and Manage Groups
>
> Modify the Membership of a Group

6. Click Next to continue, then click Finish to save the changes. Now, when the user logs on, they will be able to perform common administrative functions for all of the objects contained within the OU.

7. When finished, close the Active Directory Users and Computers tool.

Modifying User Accounts Using CSVDE

In this procedure you will use the CSVDE utility to export a list of user objects from the Active Directory. You will then make changes and then import the objects back into the Active Directory.

1. Open the Active Directory Users and Computers tool and expand the name of the Active Directory domain.

2. Create a new, top-level OU.

3. Within the OU create four users, filling in first, last, and logon names. For all other options, use the defaults.

4. Click Start ➤ Run and type **cmd** to open up a command prompt. Make a note of the current directory path because you will create an export file there for later use.

5. On a single line, type the following command to export the contents of the OU. Note that you will need to replace the OU= and DC= sections to reflect the name of your OU and current domain.

     Csvde -f export.csv -v -r "(objectclass=user)"

     ~CA-d "OU=OUName, DC=DomainName,DC=com" -m

6. Open the Active Directory Users and Computers tool. Expand the OU and delete all four users you created previously.

7. At the command prompt, type the following command:

     notepad export.csv

8. In the text file, make some changes.

9. To save the file, click File ➤ Save. For the name of the file, type **import.csv**. Make sure the Save as Type selection is All Files and the Encoding value is set to ANSI.

10. Now, to import the changed file, return to the command prompt window and type the following:

     csvde -i -f import.csv -v

11. Once you receive your results, close the command prompt.

12. To verify that the changes have been imported correctly, open the Active Directory Users and Computers tool. Within the OU right-click the field where you made changes. Verify that the changes have been made. Notice that the display name and the name displayed in the directory do not change. These are distinct attributes in the directory. When finished, close the Active Directory Users and Computers tool.

Exam Essentials

Understand how to manage Active Directory objects. Most object management is done through the Active Directory Users and Computers tool, including moving, renaming, and deleting objects.

Know how to make resources available in Active Directory. Resources are made available when they are published. The most common publishable items are printers and shared folders. Windows NT 4 resources may also be published within Active Directory.

Understand what scripting tools are used for creating users. Windows 2000 supports CSVDE, LDIFDE, and WSH scripting.

Key Terms and Concepts

Active Directory Users and Computers tool Utility used to manage objects within Active Directory.

computer objects Objects that represent individual workstations within a domain.

Comma-Separated Value Directory Exchange (CSVDE) Tool used to import and export Active Directory information from and to comma-separated value (CSV) text files.

LDIF Directory Exchange (LDIFDE) Tool used to import and export Active Directory information, similar to CSVDE. It is not designed for use with Microsoft Excel or Notepad.

printer objects   Objects representing physical print devices on your network.

publishing   The process of making resources available to users.

security principals   Objects to which security is assigned.

shared folder objects   Objects that contain files or other folders for users to access on the network.

user object   Object that represents common users of the network.

Windows Script Host (WSH)   Windows utility that allows you to create simple files that automate common functions, such as creating users.

Sample Questions

1. You cannot view the LostAndFound and System folders in the Active Directory Users and Computers tool. What does this mean?

   A. You do not have permissions to view those folders.

   B. The Advanced Options item in the View menu is unselected.

   C. Your local machine is not a domain controller.

   D. None of the above.

   Answer: B. Enabling the Advanced Options item in the View menu will allow you to see the LostAndFound and System folders.

2. Which of the following utilities creates a text file, able to be modified by standard text editors, of some or all of the objects in the Active Directory?

   A. LDIFDE

   B. CSVDE

   C. Active Directory Users and Computers

   D. None of the above

Answer: B. The CSVDE utility creates a standard text file, whereas the LDIFDE utility creates a file for use with LDIF-compatible applications.

3. How can the Windows NT 4 file and printer resources be made available from within the Active Directory?

A. You can right-click the resource and select Publish.

B. You can create Printer and Shared Folder objects that point to these resources.

C. The Active Directory Domains and Trusts tool can be used to make resources available.

D. Only Windows 2000 resources can be accessed from within the Active Directory.

Answer: B. Printer and Shared Folder objects within the Active Directory can point to Windows NT 4 file and printer resources, as well as Windows 2000 resources.

Manage Active Directory performance.

Keeping the Active Directory running at its best is an important consideration for network environments of any size. The steps involved with optimizing performance include collecting and examining performance data and then analyzing the data to locate bottlenecks.

When it comes to optimizing performance, the commonly used trial-and-error method can sometimes lead to better results, though it depends on the validity of the performance measurements you have made. Does the server just *seem* to be operating faster? If that's your only guideline, it's probably time you started collecting some hard statistics to back up that feeling! Windows 2000 comes with specific tools designed for measuring performance.

Critical Information

The first step in any performance-optimization strategy is to measure performance accurately and consistently. The insight you'll gain from monitoring factors, such as network utilization, will be extremely useful in measuring the effects of any changes.

The overall process of performance monitoring usually involves the following steps:

1. Establish a baseline of current performance.

2. Identify bottleneck(s).

3. Plan for and implement changes.

4. Measure the effects of the changes.

5. Repeat the process.

NOTE   You will never eliminate all bottlenecks in performance. The goal is to simply eliminate as many as possible.

Here are some important ideas to consider when monitoring performance:

Plan changes carefully.   When working in an easy-to-use, GUI-based operating system like the Windows 2000 platform, it's tempting to just remove a check mark here or there and then retest the performance. Don't. Before you make haphazard changes (especially on production servers), take the time to learn about, plan for, and test your changes.

Make only one change at a time.   Changing one item lets you determine exactly *which* change created the positive effects.

Ensure consistency in measurements.   Controlling variables, such as system load at various times during the day, can help. Employ a consistent monitoring schedule.

Utilize a test environment.   To avoid negative impacts on users, attempt to make as many changes as possible within a test environment. When this isn't possible, be sure to make changes during off-peak hours.

Maintain a performance history.   The performance-optimization cycle is a continuous improvement process. Because many changes may be made over time, it is important to track the changes made and the results.

Many factors influence optimal performance. The tools included with Windows 2000 can help in organizing the process and taking measurements.

Monitoring 101

The first step in monitoring performance is to decide *what* you want to monitor. In Windows 2000, hundreds of easily tracked performance statistics relate to the operating system and associated services. The performance statistics fall into three main categories:

Objects   An object within the *System Monitor* is a collection of various performance statistics you can monitor. Objects are based on areas of system resources, like the processor, memory, and services such as Web service.

Counters   *Counters* are specific items grouped within objects and are the parameters measured by the System Monitor.

Instances   Some counters will also have *instances* that further identify which performance parameter the counter is measuring. If you are monitoring two CPUs, for example, you can choose *which* CPU you are monitoring with the particular counter.

You can specify which objects, counters, and instances you want to monitor by quickly and easily adding them to the System Monitor. Figure 4.3 shows the various options available when adding new counters to the System Monitor.

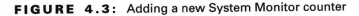

FIGURE 4.3: Adding a new System Monitor counter

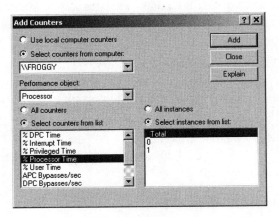

The exact items you will be able to monitor will depend on your hardware and software configuration. For example, if you have not installed and configured the Internet Information Server (IIS) service, the options available within the Web Server objects will not be available. Or, if you have multiple network adapters or CPUs in the server, you will have the option to view each instance separately or as part of the total value.

System Monitor

The Windows 2000 System Monitor was designed to show information in a clear format. Based on the type of performance information you're reviewing, however, you might want to change the display. You can choose from three main views to review statistics and information on performance:

Graph View The *Graph view* is the default display presented when you first access the Windows 2000 System Monitor. The chart shows values along the vertical axis and time along the horizontal axis.

Graph view is valuable for seeing values and changes in them over a period of time. Figure 4.4 provides an example of the Graph view.

FIGURE 4.4: Viewing information in the System Monitor Graph view

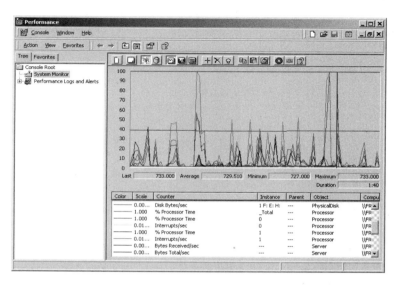

Histogram View The *Histogram view* shows performance statistics and information with a set of relative bar charts. You can utilize the Histogram to view a snapshot of the latest value for a given counter. Figure 4.5 shows a typical Histogram view.

FIGURE 4.5: Viewing information in the System Monitor Histogram view

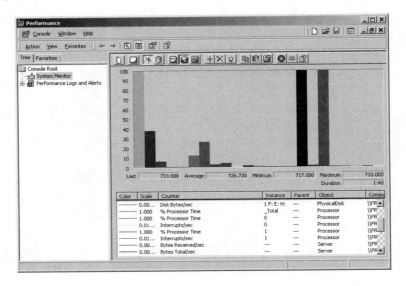

Report View Like the Histogram view, the *Report view* shows performance statistics based on the latest measurement or displays an average measurement and minimum and maximum thresholds. It is most useful for determining exact values, since it provides information in numeric terms. Figure 4.6 provides an example of the type of information you'll see in the Report view.

FIGURE 4.6: Viewing information in the System Monitor Report view

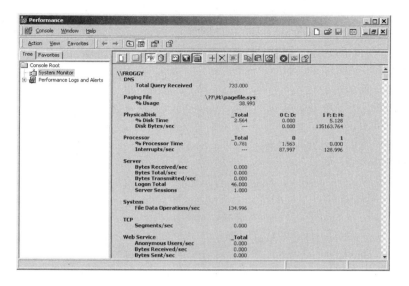

Managing System Monitor Properties

Through the System Monitor properties, you can specify additional settings for viewing performance information. You can access the options by clicking the Properties button in the task bar or by right-clicking the System Monitor display and selecting Properties. Here are the tabs:

General   In the *General tab* (shown in Figure 4.7), you can specify several options that relate to the System Monitor view. First, you can choose from among the Graph, Histogram, and Report views. Next, you can enable or disable legends, the value bar, and the toolbar.

FIGURE 4.7: General System Monitor properties

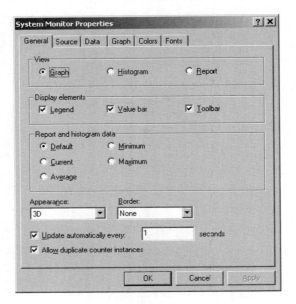

Source In the *Source tab*, you can specify the source for the performance information you would like to view. Options include current activity (the default setting) or data from a log file.

Data The *Data tab* displays a list of the counters added to the System Monitor display. The counters apply to the Chart, Histogram, and Report views.

Graph In the *Graph tab*, you can specify certain options to customize the display of the System Monitor views. Specifically, you can add a title for the graph, specify a label for the vertical axis, choose to display grids, and stipulate the vertical-scale range.

Colors Using the *Colors tab*, you can set the colors for certain areas of the display, such as background and foreground.

Fonts In the *Fonts tab*, you can indicate the fonts used to display counter values in the System Monitor views.

Performance Logs and Alerts

You need to monitor performance over a given period of time. When viewing information in the System Monitor, you have two main options with respect to the data on display:

View Current Activity   When you first open the Performance icon from the Administrative Tools folder, the default is to view data obtained from current system information. You may thus measure and display various real-time statistics on the system's performance.

View Log File Data   Alternatively, you can view information previously saved to a log file. Although the objects, counters, and instances may appear to be the same as those viewed using the *View Current Activity* option, the information was captured at a previous point in time.

TIP   Although System Monitor allows you to view network-utilization statistics, it does not let you examine individual packets. To capture and examine packets, use Network Monitor.

You create logs by accessing the Performance Logs and Alerts section of the Windows 2000 Performance tool. Once there, you'll see three types of items that allow you to customize how the data is collected in the log files:

Counter Logs   *Counter logs* record performance statistics based on the various objects, counters, and instances available in the System Monitor. The values are updated based on a time-interval setting and are saved to a file for later analysis.

Trace Logs   Some types of information are better monitored by specific events instead of the passage of specified time intervals. *Trace logs* record event-based performance information to files. Several trace-log types can be included by default:

- Windows 2000 Kernel Trace Provider
- Active Directory: Netlogon

- Active Directory: SAM

- Active Directory: Kerberos

- Windows NT Active Directory Service

- Local Security Authority (LSA)

Alerts   *Alerts* monitor the standard objects, counters, and instances available with the Windows 2000 Performance Monitoring tools. Further, they take specific actions when certain performance-statistic thresholds are exceeded. For example, you could create an alert that fires every time the CPU utilization on the local server exceeds 95 percent (as shown in Figure 4.8).

FIGURE 4.8: Setting an alert on processor utilization

You can configure various events to occur when an alert fires, like logging an entry in the application event log (which can be viewed using Event Viewer), sending a network message to a specific user or computer, starting a performance data-log operation, or running a specific program.

When saving performance information to files, there are two logging methods:

Circular Logging In *circular logging*, the data stored within a file is overwritten as new data is entered into the log. Use this method of logging if you only want to record information for a certain time frame. Circular logging conserves disk space.

Linear Logging Opposite to circular logging, *linear logging* adds information to the end of the log file without deleting. The log file continually grows, but historical information is retained.

Monitoring Domain Controller Performance

When it comes to performance, domain controllers have the same basic resource requirements as the other machines in your environment. The major areas to monitor include:

- Processor (CPU) time
- Memory
- Disk I/O
- Disk space
- Network utilization

Before implementing a monitoring plan, you should carefully determine which statistics are most useful. For example, if you're measuring the performance of a database server, CPU time and memory may be the most important—or perhaps not, considering applications servers usually have high disk I/O and network requirements. Table 4.1 provides an example of some common System Monitor objects and their corresponding counters.

The list is not by any means complete—it's just a good guideline for some of the more common items. The key to determining what to monitor is to understand the demands imposed by applications or services.

TABLE 4.1: Useful Counters for Monitoring Domain Controller Performance

Object	Counter	Notes
Memory	Available MB	Displays the number of megabytes of physical memory (RAM) available.
Memory	Pages/sec	Indicates the number of pages of memory that must be read from or written to disk per second. A high number may indicate that more memory is needed.
Network Interface	Bytes Total / Second	Measures the total number of bytes per second sent to or received by the specified network-interface card.
Network Interface	Packets Received Errors	Specifies the number of received network packets that contained errors. A high number may indicate problems with the network connection.
Network Segment	% Net Utilization	Specifies the percentage of total network resources being consumed. A high value may indicate network congestion. Note: you must have the Network Monitor agent installed on the local computer to view this counter.
Paging File	% Usage	Indicates the amount of the Windows virtual memory file (paging file) in use. If a large number, the machine may benefit from a RAM upgrade.
Physical Disk	Disk Reads / sec Disk Writes / sec	Indicates the amount of disk activity on the server.

TABLE 4.1:   Useful Counters for Monitoring Domain Controller
Performance *(continued)*

Object	Counter	Notes
Physical Disk	Avg. Disk Queue Length	Indicates the number of disk read or write requests waiting to access the disk. If high, disk I/O could be a bottleneck.
Processor	% Processor Time	Indicates the overall CPU load on the server. High values generally indicate processor-intensive tasks. In machines with multiple processors, each processor can be monitored individually, or a total value can be viewed.
Server	Bytes Total / sec	Specifies the number of bytes sent by the Server service on the local machine. A high value usually indicates the server is responsible for fulfilling many outbound data requests (such as a file/print server).
Server	Server Sessions	Indicates the number of users accessing the server.
System	Processor Queue Length	Shows the number of threads awaiting CPU time. A high number might indicate a reduction in available CPU resources is creating a bottleneck.
System	Processes	Indicates the number of processes currently running on the system.

TABLE 4.1: Useful Counters for Monitoring Domain Controller Performance *(continued)*

Object	Counter	Notes
Web Service	Bytes Total / sec	Lists the number of bytes of data transmitted to or from the local Web service. This option is only available if Internet Information Server (IIS) is installed, and the Web server is running.

Monitoring Active Directory Performance

The Windows 2000 operating system automatically tracks many performance statistics related to the Active Directory. (You can also easily access these statistics by using the System Monitor.) The specific counters are part of the NTDS object and are based on several different functions of the Active Directory, including:

- The Address Book (AB)
- The Directory Replication Agent (DRA)
- The Directory Service (DS)
- The Key Distribution Center (KDC)
- The Lightweight Directory Access Protocols (LDAP)
- The NTLM Authentications
- The Security Accounts Manager (SAM)
- The Extended Directory Services (XDS)

The counters noteworthy for you will depend on the aspects of Active Directory performance you're planning to examine. If you want to measure performance statistics related to Active Directory replication, you will probably want to monitor the Directory Replication Agent counters. If you're interested in performance loads generated by Windows NT computers, you will want to monitor NTLM Authentications and the Security Accounts Manager.

TIP   The best way to learn about System Monitor is to use it.

It is useful to have a set of performance-monitor counters saved to files so you can quickly and easily monitor the items of interest. You may want to create a System Monitor file with statistics related to database services while another file focuses on network utilization. In that way, you can quickly determine the cause of a problem without having to create a System Monitor chart from scratch.

Monitoring Active Directory Performance Using Performance Logs and Alerts

In addition to using the System Monitor of the Windows 2000 Performance tool, you can also monitor Active Directory performance statistics through Performance Logs and Alerts. By saving historical performance information, you can get a good idea of how your systems have performed over time.

Other Performance Monitoring Tools

Three other tools besides the System Monitor can be used for monitoring performance in Windows 2000: *Network Monitor*, *Event Viewer*, and *Task Manager*.

Network Monitor

Although the System Monitor is a great tool for viewing overall network performance statistics, it doesn't give you much insight into what types of network traffic are traveling on the wire. That's where the Network Monitor comes in. The utility consists of two main components, the Network Monitor Agent and the Network Monitor tool.

The Network Monitor Agent, for Windows 2000 Professional and Server computers, is installed through the Add/Remove Programs Control Panel applet. It allows for the tracking of network packets. When you install the Network Monitor Agent, you will also be able to access the Network Segment System Monitor counter, which tracks network traffic.

On Windows 2000 Server computers, you'll see the Network Monitor icon appear in the Administrative Tools program group. You can use the Network Monitor tool to capture data as it travels on your network (see Figure 4.9).

FIGURE 4.9: Viewing performance statistics using Network Monitor

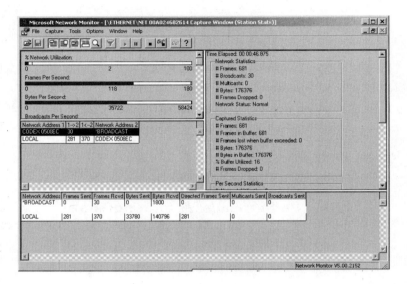

NOTE The free version of Network Monitor included with Windows 2000 Server only allows the capture of information to or from the local computer. The full version of Network Monitor comes with Systems Management Server (SMS) and places the network adapter in promiscuous mode to capture all data transferred on the network. For more information, see www.microsoft.com/management.

Once you have captured the desired data, you can save it to a capture file or further analyze it using Network Monitor. From the information you can determine how applications are communicating and the types of data passed over the network.

Task Manager

Task Manager gives you a quick snapshot of the local system. It's always readily available and does not require any configuration, like System Monitor does.

Task Manager can be easily accessed in several ways:

- Click Start ➤ Run, and type **taskmgr**.
- Right-click the Windows taskbar and then click Task Manager.
- Press Ctrl+Alt+Del and then select Task Manager.
- Press Ctrl+Shift+Esc.

Once you access the Task Manager, you will see the following three tabs:

Applications   The Applications tab shows you a list of the applications currently running on the local computer. It is a good place to check which programs are running on the system. It is also useful for shutting down any applications not responding.

Processes   The Processes tab shows you all processes currently running on the local computer. You will see the CPU time and memory for each process.

Performance   Using the Performance tab, you can view details about how memory is allocated on the computer and how much of the CPU is utilized (see Figure 4.10).

FIGURE 4.10: Viewing CPU and memory performance information using the Task Manager

Event Viewer

You can use the Event Viewer to monitor the Directory Services log, which holds information, warnings, and alerts related to the proper functioning of the directory services. An error in the Active Directory configuration preventing replication between domain controllers, for example, will leave a trail in the Directory Services log of specific events and information related to it.

In addition to the Directory Services log, Event Viewer enables you to use the application and system logs to monitor applications and other system events.

Optimizing the Active Directory

Using the Active Directory performance statistics you gather, you can identify potential bottlenecks—that is, limitations in system performance. The specific counters and acceptable values you use will be based on your specific hardware, software, network, and business requirements. In general, the System Monitor statistics help to determine if a hardware upgrade is warranted or if some configuration options should be changed. The specific changes must be evaluated based on an Active Directory subsystem.

TIP   Establish a baseline of network performance. Then, long-term deviations will scream for optimization.

Troubleshooting Active Directory Performance Monitoring

Performance monitoring uses up system resources. Therefore, you should monitor your servers from another machine, perhaps a Windows 2000 Professional workstation.

One problem: the System Monitor may not obtain performance statistics and information quickly enough. In this case increase the sample interval. The larger interval will reduce the number of statistics System Monitor has to record and display and will possibly prevent the loss of performance information.

Sometimes, when you're viewing performance information in the Chart or Histogram view, the data is either too small (the bar or line is too close to the baseline) or too large (the bar or line is above the maximum value). In either case, you'll want to adjust the scale for the counter so you can accurately see information.

Necessary Procedures

This objective has two necessary procedures: Monitoring Domain Controller and Active Directory Performance, and Using Performance Logs and Alerts.

Monitoring Domain Controller and Active Directory Performance with Windows 2000 System Monitor

In this procedure you will use features of the Windows 2000 System Monitor to analyze performance information on a Windows 2000 domain controller.

1. Open the Performance tool from the Administrative Tools program group.

2. In the left pane, right-click the System Monitor item and select Rename. Type **Domain Controller Performance** and press Enter.

3. Click the Add Counter button (the button with the "+" sign). Select Use Local Computer Counters. Choose the Processor object and then click Select Counters from List. Select the % Processor Time counter and the _Total instance. Note that you can click the Explain button to find more information about the parameters available. Click the Add button to add the counter to the chart.

4. Likewise, add other counters to the display. When you are finished adding, click the Close button.

5. Click the View Histogram button to view information. Click the counters in the bottom pane of the display to view the statistical values for last, average, minimum, and maximum.

6. Click the View Report button to view information in the Report view. Note that you will see only the latest values for each of the counters selected.

7. Click the View Chart button to return to the Graph view. Right-click the chart and select Save As. Save the chart as a Web page to a folder on the local computer. You can open this file later if you want to record information for the same counters.

8. When finished, close the Windows 2000 System Monitor.

Using Performance Logs and Alerts to Monitor Active Directory Performance

In this procedure you will use the Performance Logs and Alerts features of the Windows 2000 Performance tool to create a Counter log file, record performance statistics, and later analyze this information using the System Monitor. In order to complete the steps in this procedure, you must have first completed the last procedure.

1. Open the Performance tool from the Administrative Tools program group.

2. Under Performance Logs and Alerts, right-click Counter Logs and select New Log Settings From. Select the file you created in the previous procedure.

3. You will see a warning notifying you some settings will be set at their defaults. Click OK to continue.

4. Type the name of the new counter log and click OK. You will see the default counters from the System Monitor settings automatically added to this counter log. On the General tab, set the refresh interval to one second.

5. Click the Log Files tab. Verify that the log-file name and location are appropriate. Also, note that you have an option to automatically generate log-file names. Leave the default setting at nnnnnn and the start number at one. Change the log file type to Binary Circular File and verify that the log file size is limited to 1000KB.

6. Click the Schedule tab and select Manually (Using the Shortcut Menu) for both the Start Log and Stop Log options. Leave all other settings at their defaults.

7. Click OK to create the counter log.

8. To start recording data for the counter log, right-click the Domain Controller Log item in the right windowpane and select Start. You will notice the icon turns green. If your computer is not actively working (such as one in a test environment), you can simulate activity by running applications and searching the Active Directory.

9. Wait at least two minutes for the data collection to occur and then right-click the Domain Controller Log item and select Stop. The icon will turn red.

10. Click the System Monitor in the left pane, and click the View Log File Data button. Select the file named Domain_Controller_Log_ 000001.log from the directory in which you stored the counter data, and click Open. The Graph view will automatically be populated.

11. To filter the values displayed, right-click the chart and select Properties. On the Source tab, change the Time Range values to view only a specific amount of data. Note that you can only choose times that are within the sampling interval. Click OK to restrict the data.

12. Examine the Chart, Histogram, and Report views. When finished, close the System Monitor.

Exam Essentials

Understand what the System Monitor is used for. System Monitor allows you to monitor the performance characteristics of hardware and software on your computer or another computer.

Know what logs and alerts are used for. Logs are used for establishing baselines of performance, and for tracking changes in system performance over a period of time. Alerts are useful for warning you if a certain performance threshold has been exceeded.

Understand what Network Monitor does. Whereas System Monitor is used to analyze performance data, Network Monitor is designed to capture and analyze packets on your network. Keep in mind that the Network Monitor that comes with Windows 2000 is only capable of capturing packets sent to or from that machine's NIC. In order to monitor all network traffic, you must get an additional product, like Microsoft's SMS.

Key Terms and Concepts

alerts   Part of System Monitor designed to take specific actions when certain performance-statistic thresholds are exceeded.

baseline   The initial measurement of a component's performance or capacity characteristics, which is used to measure future contrasting measurements.

Event Viewer   Used to log any information, warnings, or alerts related to the proper functioning of directory services, applications, and system processes.

Network Monitor   Windows 2000 monitoring tool designed for the capturing and analysis of packets.

Performance logs   Long-term views of system-performance data. Used to establish a baseline of system performance.

System Monitor   Windows 2000 monitoring tool that allows you to monitor hardware and software performance statistics for your computer.

Task Manager   Basic diagnostic utility that allows you to see what applications and processes are running, and basic performance statistics on the CPU and memory.

Trace logs   System-monitor logs that record event-based performance information—rather than time-based information—to files.

Sample Questions

1. You suspect one or more computers are generating excessive PING traffic on the network. Which of the following tools can you use to determine which computers are causing the problem?

   A. Task Manager

   B. System Monitor

   C. Event Viewer

D. Network Monitor

E. None of the above

Answer: D. Through the use of the Network Monitor application, you can view all of the network packets being sent to or from the local server. Based on this information, you can determine the source of certain types of traffic, such as PINGs.

2. You want to configure the operating system to generate an item in the Windows 2000 event log whenever the CPU utilization for the server exceeds 95 percent. Which of the following items within the Performance tool can you use?

A. System Monitor

B. Trace logs

C. Counter logs

D. Alerts

E. All of the above

Answer: D. Alerts fire in response to certain performance-related parameters, as defined by systems administrators. You can configure an alert to perform several different types of actions, including writing to the Windows 2000 event log.

3. You suspect the amount of RAM in a domain controller is insufficient and an upgrade is required. Which of the following System Monitor counters would provide the most useful information regarding the upgrade?

A. Network Segment ➤ % Utilization

B. Memory ➤ Page Faults / sec

C. Processor ➤ % Utilization

D. System ➤ Processes

E. All of the above would be equally useful

Answer: B. A page fault occurs when the operating system must retrieve information from disk instead of from RAM. If the number of page faults per second is high, then it is likely that the server would benefit from a RAM upgrade.

Manage and troubleshoot Active Directory replication.

Active Directory sites are generally used to define groups of computers located within a single geographic location. In most organizations machines located in close physical proximity (for example, within a single building or branch office) are well connected.

Often, however, domain controllers are located across states, countries, and even continents. In such a situation, network connectivity is usually much slower, less reliable, and more costly than for the equivalent LAN. Therefore, Active Directory replication must accommodate accordingly.

Critical Information

When managing replication traffic within Active Directory sites, two main areas of synchronization exist: *Intrasite replication* and *Intersite replication*.

Intrasite Replication

Intrasite replication refers to the synchronization of Active Directory information between domain controllers located in the same site. As you would expect with sites, these machines are usually well connected by a high-speed LAN.

Intrasite replication is generally a simple process. One domain controller contacts the others in the same site when changes to its copy of the Active Directory are made. It compares the logical sequence numbers in its own copy of the Active Directory with that of the other domain controllers. Then the most current information is chosen, and all domain controllers within the site use this information to make the necessary updates to their database.

Because it is assumed the domain controllers within an Active Directory site are well connected, less attention to exactly when and how replication takes place is required. Communications between domain controllers occur using the *Remote Procedure Call (RPC) protocol*, which is optimized for transmitting and synchronizing information on fast and reliable network connections. The actual directory-synchronizing information is not compressed. Therefore, it provides for fast replication at the expense of network bandwidth.

Intersite Replication

Intersite replication occurs between domain controllers in different sites, usually with a WAN or other type of costly network connection between the machines. Intersite replication is optimized for minimizing the amount of network traffic between sites; that is, it fits for low-bandwidth situations and network connections that have less reliability.

Intersite replication offers several specific features tailored toward distant connections. The two protocols described subsequently may be used to transfer information between sites.

Internet Protocol (IP)

When connectivity is fairly reliable, the *Internet Protocol* is a good choice. IP-based communications require a live connection between two or more domain controllers in different sites and allow for the transfer of Active Directory information. IP was originally designed for slower WANs in which packet loss and corruption may occur often. As such, it is a good choice for low-quality connections involved in intersite replication.

Simple Mail Transfer Protocol (SMTP)

Simple Mail Transfer Protocol (SMTP) is perhaps best known as the protocol used to send e-mail messages on the Internet. SMTP uses a store-and-forward mechanism through which a server receives a copy of a message, records it to disk, and then attempts to forward it to another mail server. If the destination server is unavailable, it will hold the message and attempt to resend it at periodic intervals.

This type of communication is extremely useful for situations in which network connections are unreliable or not always available. If, for instance, a branch office in Peru were connected to the corporate office by a dial-up connection available only during certain hours, SMTP would be a good choice.

WARNING   SMTP is an inherently insecure network protocol. Therefore, you must take advantage of Windows 2000's Certificate Services if you use SMTP for Active Directory replication.

Another intersite replication characteristic designed to address low-bandwidth situations and less-reliable network connections is Active Directory–information compression. Intersite replication topology is determined through site links and site-link bridges and can occur based on a schedule defined by systems administrators.

NOTE   For information on site links and site bridges, see Chapter 1.

You can configure intersite replication through the Active Directory Sites and Services tool. Select the name of the site for which you want to configure settings. Then, right-click the NTDS Site Settings object in the right windowpane and select Properties. By clicking the Change Schedule button, you'll be able to configure how often replication between sites will occur (see Figure 4.11).

FIGURE 4.11: Configuring intersite replication schedules

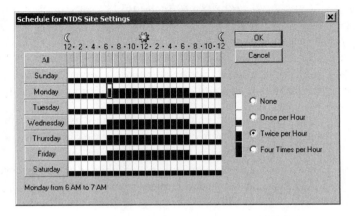

Necessary Procedures

There are no specific necessary procedures for this objective. However, to familiarize yourself with site replication, review the necessary procedures in Chapter 1 for creating site links, site-link bridges, and connection objects.

Exam Essentials

Understand the differences between intrasite and intersite replication. Intrasite replication happens within one local site, whereas intersite replication happens between sites. Intersite replication uses slower WAN links and has more configuration options.

Know what protocols are used in intersite replication and when to use each one. The protocols available for intersite replication are IP and SMTP. IP is less suitable than SMTP for unreliable links, such as dial-up, but provides for security. If you are using SMTP, you must also configure Certificate Services.

Key Terms and Concepts

Internet Protocol (IP)   Industry-standard protocol used for connection between computers. Also used for intersite replication.

intersite replication   Replication of domain-controller information between multiple logical sites.

intrasite replication   Replication of domain-controller information within one site.

Local Area Network (LAN)   Network of computers generally in one location.

Remote Procedure Call (RPC) protocol   Protocol used for intrasite replication.

Active Directory replication   The process of ensuring all Active Directory information is on all domain controllers.

Simple Mail Transfer Protocol (SMTP)   Protocol used primarily for Internet mail; it is also used for intersite replication in a Windows 2000 environment.

site   Logical grouping of computers. Usually defined by physical boundaries or separated by slow network connections.

Wide Area Network (WAN)   A collection of more than one Local Area Network. May span large geographical distances.

Sample Questions

1. Which of the following replication mechanisms uses a store-and-forward method for transferring replication data?

A. IP

B. SMTP

C. RPC

D. DHCP

E. None of the above

Answer: B. The Simple Mail Transfer Protocol (SMTP) was designed for environments in which persistent connections may not always be available. SMTP uses the store-and-forward method to ensure that information is not lost if a connection cannot be made.

2. Which of the following protocols may be used for intrasite replication?

   A. RPC

   B. IP

   C. SMTP

   D. NNTP

   E. Both B and C

   Answer: A. Remote Procedure Calls (RPCs) are used for intrasite replication.

Chapter

5

Configuring, Managing, Monitoring, and Troubleshooting Active Directory Security Solutions

MICROSOFT EXAM OBJECTIVES COVERED IN THIS CHAPTER:

Configure and troubleshoot security in a directory services infrastructure. *(pages 230 – 246)*

- Apply security policies by using Group Policy.
- Create, analyze, and modify security configurations by using Security Configuration and Analysis and Security Templates.
- Implement an audit policy.

Monitor and analyze security events. *(pages 246 – 251)*

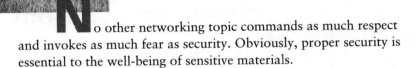

No other networking topic commands as much respect and invokes as much fear as security. Obviously, proper security is essential to the well-being of sensitive materials.

If security is too tight, people can't do their jobs. You will hear about it. If security is too loose, important files may be destroyed. Or employees may have access to the company salary file, or someone may send the boss hate mail on your behalf. With such security breeches, you may end up flipping burgers.

Group Policies help administer security on a large scale and virtually eliminates the need for managing resources on a user-by-user basis.

Once a network is set up, you should implement a rigorous auditing schedule. Through auditing and analyzing security events (like someone trying to hack in as the Administrator), you can head off potential problems.

Configure and troubleshoot security in a directory services infrastructure.

One of the systems administrator's primary responsibilities is security management. With Active Directory tools, you can define fundamental security objects through the Users, Groups, and Computers security principals. Then you can allow or disallow access to resources by granting specific *permissions* to each object.

TIP Proper planning for security permissions is as crucial as the actual implementation.

If your security settings are too restrictive, users may not be able to adequately perform their jobs. Worse yet, they may try to circumvent security measures. At the other end of the spectrum, if security permissions are too lax, users may be able to access and modify sensitive company resources.

Critical Information

One of the design goals for the Active Directory is to define a single, centralized repository of users and information resources. The Active Directory records information about all users, computers, and resources on your network. Each domain acts as a security boundary, and members of the domain (including workstations, servers, and domain controllers) share information about the objects within them.

The information stored within the Active Directory also determines which resources are accessible to which users. Through permissions assigned to Active Directory objects, you can control all aspects of network security.

Security Principals

Security principals are Active Directory objects assigned security identifiers (SIDs). A SID is a unique identifier used to manage any object to which permissions can be assigned. Security principals are assigned permissions to perform certain actions and access certain network resources.

The basic types of Active Directory objects that serve as security principals are:

User Accounts   These objects identify individual users on your network. The user account includes information such as the user's name and password.

Groups   Groups are used to combine users based on functionality. Instead of assigning permissions to users, assigning them to groups makes administration easier.

Computer Accounts   Computer accounts identify which client computers are members of particular domains. Because these computers participate in the Active Directory database, you can manage security settings that affect the computer. Computer accounts are used to determine whether a computer can join a domain and for authentication purposes.

Security principals can be assigned permissions so they can access various network resources and be given user rights. They may also have their actions tracked through *auditing*. The three types of security principals—users, groups, and computers—form the basis of the Active Directory security architecture.

A unique SID defines each security principal, so deleting a security principal is an irreversible process. For example, if you delete a user account and then later re-create one with the same name, you will need to reassign permissions and group-membership settings for the new account.

Other objects—such as organizational units (OUs)—do not function as security principals. Therefore, whereas you can apply certain settings (such as Group Policy) on all objects within an OU, you cannot set permissions on the OU itself. The purpose of OUs is to logically organize other Active Directory objects based on business needs. The distinction is important.

Understanding Users and Groups

The two fundamental security principals used for security administration are users and groups.

Types of Groups

When dealing with groups, you should make the distinction between local security principals and domain security principals. Local users and groups are used for assigning the permissions necessary to access the local machine. For example, you may assign the permissions necessary to restart a domain controller to a specific local group. Domain users and groups, however, are used throughout the domain. The local and domain objects are available on any of the computers within the Active Directory domain and between domains with a trust relationship.

Two main types of Groups are used in the Active Directory:

Security Groups   *Security groups* are considered security principals and can contain User accounts. To make administration simpler, assign permissions to groups. Active Directory Contact objects can also be placed within Security groups, but security permissions will not apply to them.

Distribution Groups   *Distribution groups* are not considered security principals and are used only for the purpose of sending e-mail messages. You add users to Distribution groups just as you would add them to Security groups. Distribution groups can also be placed within OUs for easier management.

When working in native-mode domains (domains that support the use of only Windows 2000 domain controllers), Security groups can be converted to Distribution groups. When running in mixed mode (which allows the use of Windows NT domain controllers), group types cannot be changed.

Group Scope

In addition to being classified by type, each group is also given a specific scope. The scope of a Group defines two characteristics. First, it determines the level of security that applies to a group. Second, it determines which users can be added to the group. Group scope ultimately defines which resources users will be able to access.

The three types of group scopes are:

Domain Local   The scope of *Domain Local groups* extends no farther than the local machine. When you're using the Active Directory Users and Computers tool, Domain Local accounts apply to the computer for which you are viewing information. Domain Local groups are used to assign permissions to local resources such as files and printers. They can contain *Global groups, Universal groups,* and user accounts.

Global   The scope of Global groups is limited to a single domain. Global groups may contain any users that are part of the Active Directory domain in which the Global groups reside.

Universal   Universal groups can contain users from any domain within an Active Directory forest. Therefore, they are used for managing security across domains. When managing multiple domains, group Global groups within Universal groups.

TIP   Universal groups are only available when you're running the Active Directory in native mode.

Each of these scope levels is designed for a specific purpose and will ultimately affect the types of security permissions that can be assigned to them.

In order to process authentication between domains, information about the membership in Universal groups is stored in the Global Catalog (GC). Keep this in mind if you ever plan to place users directly into Universal groups and bypass Global groups. All users will be enumerated in the GC, which will impact size and performance.

The properties for each of these group types are affected by whether Active Directory is running in mixed mode or native mode. Several limitations on group functionality exist when running in mixed-mode domains:

- Only Distribution groups can have Universal scope. Universal security groups are not available in mixed-mode domains.

- Changing the scope of groups is not allowed.

- The only group nesting allowed is Global groups contained in Domain Local groups.

When running in native-mode domains, you can make the following Group scope changes:

- Domain Local groups can be changed to a Universal group, but only if the Domain Local group does not contain any other Domain Local groups.

- A Global group can be changed to a Universal group, but only if the Global group is not a member of any other Global groups.

Universal groups themselves cannot be converted into any other Group scope type.

Built-In Local Groups

Built-in local groups are used for performing administrative functions on the local server. Because they have preassigned permissions and privileges, they allow you to easily assign common management functions. The list of built-in local groups includes:

Account Operators   These users are able to create and modify Domain User and Group accounts. Members of this group are generally responsible for the daily administration of the Active Directory.

Administrators   Members of the *Administrators group* are given full permissions to perform any functions within the Active Directory domain and on the local computer. Members can access all files and resources that reside on any server with the domain.

TIP   Restrict the number of users in the Administrators group; most common administration functions do not require this level of access.

Backup Operators   Members of the *Backup Operators group* can bypass standard file-system security for the purpose of backup and recovery only. They cannot directly access or open files within the file system.

Guests   The *Guests group* is essentially used for providing access to resources that generally do not require security. For example, you can allow members of the Guest group to access files that are accessible to all network users.

Print Operators   Members of the *Print Operators group* are given permissions to administer all of the printers within a domain. They can change the priority of print jobs, delete items from the print queue, and perform other common print functions.

Replicator   The *Replicator group* was created to allow the replication of files between the computers in a domain. Accounts used for replication-related tasks are added to this group to provide them with the permissions necessary to keep files synchronized across multiple computers.

Server Operators A common administrative task is managing server configuration. Members of the *Server Operators group* are granted the permissions necessary to manage services, shares, and other system settings.

Users The Users group is often used as a generic grouping for network accounts. Usually, this group is given minimal permissions and is used for the application of security settings that apply to most employees within an organization.

TIP Before taking the test, familiarize yourself with the functionality of each built-in group.

Additionally, two main user accounts are created during the promotion of a domain controller. The first is the *Administrator account*. This account is assigned the password provided by a systems administrator during the promotion process and has full permissions to perform all actions within the domain. The second is *Guest account*, which is disabled by default. The purpose of the Guest account is to provide anonymous access to users who do not have an individual logon and password for use within the domain. It is generally recommended that the Guest account be disabled to increase security.

Predefined Global Groups

Global groups are used for managing permissions at the domain level. The following predefined Global groups are installed in the Users folder:

Cert Publishers Certificates increase security by allowing for strong authentication methods. User accounts are placed within the *Cert Publishers group* if they require the ability to publish security certificates. Generally, these accounts will be used by Active Directory security services.

Domain Computers Generally, all computers of the domain are members of the *Domain Computers group*. Membership includes any workstations or servers that have joined the domain but does not include the domain controllers.

Domain Admins   Members of the *Domain Admins* group have full permissions to manage all Active Directory objects for the domain. Membership should be restricted to only those users who require full permissions.

Domain Controllers   Normally, all domain controllers for a given domain are included within the *Domain Controllers group*.

Domain Guests   Members of the *Domain Guests group* are usually given minimal permissions with respect to resources. You may place User accounts in this group if they require only basic access or require temporary permissions within the domain.

Domain Users   The *Domain Users group* typically contains all user accounts for the given domain. This group is generally given basic permissions to resources that do not require higher levels of security.

Enterprise Admins   Members of the *Enterprise Admins group* are given full permissions to perform actions within the entire domain forest. Members can manage trust relationships and add new domains to trees and forests.

Group Policy Creator Owners   Members of the *Group Policy Creator Owners group* are able to create and modify Group Policy settings for objects within the domain. They can enable security settings on OUs and the objects that OUs contain.

Schema Admins   Members of the *Schema Admins group* are given permissions to modify the Active Directory schema. Therefore, they can, for example, create additional fields of information for User accounts.

TIP   As with local groups, know who default members of global groups are and what they can do.

Groups other than those listed above might be created for specific services and applications installed on the server. Specifically, services that run on domain controllers and servers will be created as security groups with Domain Local scope. As an example, installing the DHCP service creates the *DHCPUsers* and *DHCPAdministrators* groups.

Foreign Security Principals

In environments that consist of more than one domain, you may need to grant permissions to users who reside in multiple domains. Generally, you would use Active Directory trees and forests. However, in some cases you may want to provide resources to users not part of the same forest.

The Active Directory uses *Foreign security principals* to allow permissions to be assigned to users not part of the same Active Directory forest. The process is automatic and does not require the intervention of systems administrators. The Foreign security principals can then be added to Domain Local groups, which can be granted permissions for resources within the domain.

Managing Security and Permissions

The general practice for managing security is to assign users to groups and then grant permissions to the groups so they can access certain resources.

For ease of management and to implement a hierarchical structure, you can place groups within OUs. You can also assign Group Policy settings to all of the objects contained within an OU. By using this method, you can combine the benefits of a hierarchical structure (through OUs) and the use of security principals.

The primary tool used to manage security permissions for Users, Groups, and Computers is the Active Directory Users and Computers snap-in. Here are some of the tasks you can perform with this tool:

- Reset a user's password
- Create new user accounts

- Modify group memberships based on changes in job requirements and functions

- Disable user accounts

Permissions

Once you've properly grouped your users, you'll need to set the permissions that will affect the objects within the Active Directory. The permissions available will vary based on the type of object. The following shows some permissions that can be applied to various Active Directory objects and explains what each permission does:

- *Control Access* changes security permissions on the object.

- *Create Child* creates objects within an OU (such as other OUs).

- *Delete Child* deletes child objects within an OU.

- *Delete Tree* deletes an OU and the objects within it.

- *List Contents* shows objects within an OU.

- *List Object* lists objects within an OU.

- *Read* shows properties of an object (such as a user name).

- *Write* modifies properties of an object.

Using Group Policy for Security

Through the use of the Active Directory, you can define Group Policy objects and then apply them to OUs. The settings you specify will apply to all security principals included within the OU to which the Group Policy applies.

Using the Security Configuration and Analysis Utility

In order to make the creation and application of security settings easier, Microsoft has included the *Security Configuration and Analysis tool* with Windows 2000. With the tool you can create, modify, and apply security settings in the Registry through the use of Security Template files. *Security Templates* allow you to define security settings once and then store the information in a file that can be applied to other computers.

The Template file provides a description of the settings, along with information about the Registry key(s) to which the modifications must be made. Templates can be applied to both users and computers.

The overall process for working with the Security Configuration and Analysis tool is:

1. Open or create a Security Database file.

2. Import an existing Template file.

3. Analyze the local computer.

4. Make setting changes, if necessary.

5. Save any template changes.

6. Export the new template (optional).

7. Apply the changes to the local computer (optional).

There is no default icon for the Security Configuration and Analysis tool. In order to access it, you must manually choose the snap-in from within the Microsoft Management Console (MMC) tool.

If any errors occurred during the Security Configuration and Analysis process, the results will be stored in the Log file created. Be sure to examine it for any errors in your configuration.

Necessary Procedures

The first of three necessary procedures for this objective has you create users and groups and practice managing them. Then, you get to apply security settings using Group Policy. Finally, you will use the Security Configuration and Analysis tool.

Creating and Managing Users and Groups

In this procedure you will create Users and Groups within the Active Directory and then place users into groups.

1. Open the Active Directory Users and Computers tool.

2. Create a few top-level OUs.

3. Create the several User objects within different OUs.

4. Right-click an OU and select New ➢ Group. Choose a name for the group and specify Global for the group scope and Security for the group type. Click OK to create the group.

5. To assign users to the group, right-click the group object and select Properties. Change to the Members tab and click Add. From the list select a few users and then click OK. You will see the group membership. Click OK to finish adding the users to the group.

6. When finished creating users and groups, close the Active Directory Users and Computers tool.

Applying Security Policies by Using Group Policy

In this procedure you will assign security permissions by using Group Policy. In order to complete the steps of this procedure, you must have completed the previous procedure.

1. Open the Active Directory Users and Computers tool.

2. Right-click an OU and select Properties.

3. Change to the Group Policy tab, and click New. Type the name of the new Group Policy.

4. To specify the Group Policy settings, click Edit.

5. In the Group Policy window, open Computer Configuration ➢ Windows Settings ➢ Security Settings ➢ Account Policies ➢ Password Policy object.

6. In the right-hand pane, double-click the Minimum Password Length setting. In the window, place a check mark next to the Define This Policy Setting option. Leave the default value of 7 characters. Click OK.

7. Open User Configuration ➢ Administrative Templates ➢ Control Panel object. Double-click Disable Control Panel, select Enabled, and then click OK.

8. Close the Group Policy window to save the settings you chose. Click OK and Close to enable the Security Group Policy for the OU.

9. To view the security permissions for a Group Policy object, right-click the OU and select Properties. On the Group Policy tab, highlight the Group Policy object with the name of the new Group Policy and select Properties.

10. Select the Security tab. Click Add and select a user from the list. Click Add and OK. Highlight the user and allow Read and Write permissions.

11. Click OK twice to save the changes. The user will now be able to view and change information for objects in the OU.

12. When finished, close the Active Directory Users and Computers tool.

Using the Security Configuration and Analysis Utility

In this procedure you will use the Security Configuration and Analysis utility to create and modify security configurations.

1. Click Start ➢ Run, type **mmc**, and press Enter to open a blank MMC.

2. In the Console menu, select Add/Remove Snap-In. Click Add. Select the Security Configuration and Analysis item and then click Add. Click Close.

3. You will see that the Security Configuration and Analysis snap-in has been added to the configuration. Click OK to continue.

4. Within the MMC right-click Security Configuration and Analysis and select Open Database. Change to a local directory on your computer, and create a new Security Database file. Note the location of this file, as you'll need it in later steps. Click OK.

5. Next, you'll be prompted to open a Security Template file. By default, such files are stored within the Security\Templates directory of your Windows NT system root. From the list select DC Security and place a check mark in the Clear This Database before Importing box. Click Open to load the Template file.

6. Now that you have created a Security Database file and opened a template, you can start performing useful security tasks. Notice that several tasks will be available. To perform an analysis on the security configuration of the local computer, right-click the Security Configuration and Analysis utility, and select Analyze Computer Now. When prompted, enter the path to a local directory with the filename of the Security Database file. Click OK to begin the analysis process.

7. You will see the Security Configuration and Analysis utility begin to analyze your computer.

8. When the process has been completed, you will be able to view the current security settings for the local computer. Navigate through the items to view the current security configuration.

9. To make changes to this template, expand the Password Policy object under the Account Policies object. Double-click the Enforce Password History item. Place a check mark next to the Define This Policy in the Database option and type a number for Passwords Remembered. Click OK to make the setting change. Note that this change in setting was not enabled for the local computer—the change was implemented only within the Security Database file.

10. To save the changes to the Security Database file, right-click the Security and Configuration Analysis object and select Save.

11. To export the current settings to a Template file, right-click the Security and Configuration Analysis object and select Export Template. You will be prompted for the location and filename to which these settings should be saved. Be sure to choose a meaningful name so other systems administrators will understand the purpose of this template.

12. The configuration change you made has not yet been applied to any machines. To apply the change to the local computer, right-click the Security and Configuration Analysis object and select Configure Computer Now. You will be prompted to enter the path for a Log file. Enter any path on the local computer and specify the filename of the Security Database file. Click OK. You will see the settings being applied to the local computer.

13. To quickly view the contents of the Log file for the most recent operation, right-click the Security and Configuration Analysis object and select View Log.

14. When you are finished, exit the Security and Configuration Analysis tool by closing the MMC.

Exam Essentials

Understand how group scope affects security. The scope of the group ultimately determines its security. Groups with a universal scope have a much greater range of security possibilities than a Domain Local scope.

Understand the difference between Security groups and Distribution groups. Security groups contain security principals, which are assigned permissions to resources. Distribution groups are used for e-mail purposes only.

Know the different built-in local and global groups, who are members by default, and what their functions are. If you are unfamiliar with these, please review the objective.

Key Terms and Concepts

Distribution groups Groups within Active Directory used for managing e-mail. They are not used for assigning permissions.

Domain Local groups Scope in which group accounts apply to the computer for which you are viewing information.

Foreign security principals Allow permissions to be assigned to users not part of the same Active Directory forest.

Global groups Groups that may contain any users who are part of the Active Directory domain.

permissions Grant users the ability to access resources.

Security Configuration and Analysis utility   Tool used to create, modify, and apply security settings in the Registry through the use of Security Template files.

Security groups   Groups used for easing the assigning and management of security permissions.

Security principals   Objects to which permissions can be assigned.

Security templates   Allow you to define security settings once and then store this information in a file that can be applied to other computers.

Universal groups   Group scope that applies to all possible users within your domain or tree.

Sample Questions

1. Which of the following types of groups can contain other groups when operating in native mode?

   A. Universal groups

   B. Domain Local groups

   C. Global groups

   D. Distribution groups

   E. All of the above

   Answer: E. All of these types of groups can contain other groups when operating in native mode.

2. Which of the following features of the Security Configuration and Analysis tool helps systems administrators apply uniform security policies to users and computers?

   A. Security descriptors

   B. Domain policies

C. Security templates

D. All of the above

Answer: C. Through the use of templates, the Security Configuration and Analysis tool allows systems administrators to define various configuration settings and then apply them to users and computers.

3. Members of which of the following built-in local groups are able to bypass file-system security for specific functions?

A. Account Operators

B. Backup Operators

C. Guests

D. Domain Administrators

E. None of the above

Answer: B. Members of the Backup Operators Local group are able to bypass file-system security in order to back up and restore files, though they cannot directly access or open the files.

Monitor and analyze security events.

One of the most important aspects of controlling security in networked environments is ensuring that only authorized users are able to access specific resources. Even though you spend much time in managing security permissions, it is almost always possible for a security problem to occur. Sometimes, the best way to find possible security breaches is to actually record the actions taken by specific users. Then, in the case of a security breach, you can examine the log to find the cause of the problem. The Windows 2000 operating system and the Active Directory offer the ability to audit a wide range of actions.

Critical Information

Auditing involves recording specific actions. From a security standpoint, auditing detects any possible misuse of network resources. Although auditing will not necessarily prevent the misuse of resources, it will help determine when security violations occurred or were attempted.

You will need to complete several steps in order to implement auditing using Windows 2000:

- Configure the size and storage settings for the audit logs.

- Enable categories of events to audit.

- Specify which objects and actions should be recorded in the audit log.

Note that there are trade-offs to implementing auditing. First and foremost, recording auditing information can decrease overall system performance and use up valuable disk space. Secondly, auditing many events can make the audit log impractical to view. If too much detail is provided, you are unlikely to scrutinize all recorded events.

Implementing Auditing

Auditing is not an all-or-none process. As is the case with security in general, you must choose which specific objects and actions you want to audit.

The main categories for auditing include:

- Account logon events

- Account management

- Directory-service access

- Logon events

- Object access

- Policy change

- Privilege use
- Process tracking
- System events

In order to audit access to objects stored within the Active Directory, you must enable the Audit Directory Service Access option. Then, you must specify which objects and actions should be tracked.

Viewing Auditing Information

One of the most important aspects of auditing is regularly monitoring the audit logs. If this step is ignored, the auditing is useless. Windows 2000 includes the *Event Viewer* tool that allows you to view audited events. Using the filtering capabilities of Event Viewer, you can find specific events of interest.

Necessary Procedures

For this objective you will enable auditing of objects, enable auditing of a specific OU, and analyze a security log in Event Viewer.

Enabling Auditing of Active Directory Objects

In this procedure you will enable auditing for an Active Directory domain. In order to complete the steps in this procedure, you must have already completed the first procedure for the last objective.

1. Open the Domain Controller Security Policy tool.

2. Expand Security Settings ➤ Local Policies ➤ Audit Policy.

3. Double-click the setting for Audit Directory Service Access. Place a check mark next to the options for Define These Policy Settings, Success, and Failure. Click OK to save the settings.

4. Expand Security Settings ➤ Event Log ➤ Settings for Event Logs to see the options associated with the event logs.

5. Double-click the Maximum Security Log Size item and set the value to 2048KB. Click OK.

6. Double-click the Retain Security Log Setting item and specify that events should be overwritten after seven days. Click OK. You will be notified that the Retention Method for Security Log option will also be changed. Click OK to accept the changes.

7. When you are finished enabling auditing options, close the Domain Controller Security Configuration tool.

Enabling Auditing for a Specific OU

In this procedure you will enable auditing for an OU. In order to complete the steps in this procedure, you must have completed the last procedure.

1. Open the Active Directory Users and Computers tool.

2. To enable auditing for an object, right-click an OU and select Properties. Select the Group Policy Tab.

3. Highlight a Group Policy object, and select Properties. Select the Security tab, and then click Advanced. Select the Auditing tab. You will see the current auditing settings for the Group Policy object.

4. Click the View/Edit button. Notice that you can view and change audit settings based on the objects and/or properties. To retain the current settings, click OK. To exit the configuration for the object, click OK three more times.

5. When you are finished with the auditing settings, close the Active Directory Users and Computers tool.

Generating and Viewing Audit Logs

In this procedure you will perform some actions that will be audited, and then you will view the information recorded within the audit logs. In order to complete this procedure, you must have completed the last procedure.

1. Open the Active Directory Users and Computers tool.

2. Within an OU right-click a user account and select Properties. Add or change the middle initial for the user account and specify a title in the Description box. Click OK to save the changes.

3. Within the OU right-click another user account and select Properties. Add or change a description and click OK.

4. Close the Active Directory Users and Computers tool.

5. Open the Event Viewer tool from the Administrative Tools program group. Select the Security Log item.

6. You will see a list of audited events categorized under Directory Service Access. Note that you can obtain more details about a specific item by double-clicking it.

7. To modify the Log File settings, in the right-hand pane of the Computer Management window, right-click the Directory Service item and choose Properties. Change the value for the Maximum Log File Size to 2048KB, and select the Overwrite Events as Needed option. The setting will allow you to store more audit events in the log and will ensure that events are cleared out of the log as needed. To save the new settings, click OK.

8. When you are finished viewing the security log, close the Computer Management tool.

Exam Essentials

Understand what auditing is used for, and the advantages and disadvantages of it.   Auditing is used for tracking system events, such as when people log on and off or access files. The advantage is increased security. The major disadvantage is it requires ample system resources.

Key Terms and Concepts

auditing   The process of tracking and recording various events on a computer.

Sample Questions

1. Which of the following is used to enable auditing for Active Directory objects?

   A. Computer Management tool

   B. Active Directory Users and Computers tool

   C. Active Directory Domains and Trusts tool

   D. Event Viewer tool

   E. All of the above

   Answer: B. The Active Directory Users and Computers tool allows systems administrators to change auditing options and to choose which actions are audited.

2. Which of the following statements regarding auditing and the Active Directory is false?

   A. Auditing prevents users from attempting to guess passwords.

   B. Systems administrators should regularly review audit logs for suspicious activity.

   C. Auditing information can be generated when users view specific information within the Active Directory.

   D. Auditing information can be generated when users modify specific information within the Active Directory.

   E. All of the above

   Answer: A. The purpose of auditing is to monitor and record actions taken by users. Auditing will not prevent users from attempting to guess passwords, although it might discourage them from trying if they are aware it is enabled.

Index

Note to the Reader: Page numbers in **bold** indicate the principal discussion of a topic or the definition of a term. Page numbers in *italic* indicate illustrations.

finding objects, 184, 194–195
folders
   directory shares for application
     deployment, 134–135, 144
   LostAndFound folder, 181–182
Fonts tab in System Monitor Properties
   dialog box, 206
Force Policy Inheritance setting for
   Group Policy Objects, 111–112,
   115
foreign security principals, 180, 238,
   244
forests, 21, 46
forward-lookup zones, 76–79, 89–90,
   91–92, 93
forwarders, 81, 93
FQDNs (Fully Qualified Domain
   Names), 66–67
Fully Qualified Domain Names
   (FQDNs), 66–67

G

General tab
   in Software Installation Properties
     dialog box, 137–138, *137*
   in System Monitor Properties dialog
     box, 205, *206*
   in zone Properties dialog box, 76, *77*
Global Catalog (GC)
   domain trees and, 22–23, 47
   Global Catalog servers, 25–26, 42
   Universal groups and, 234
Global groups
   defined, **233**, **244**
   predefined Global groups, 236–238
Global Unique Identifiers (GUIDs), **152**,
   168
GPOs. *See* Group Policies
Graph tab in System Monitor Properties
   dialog box, 206
Graph view in System Monitor, 202–
   203, *203*
Group objects, **12**

Group Policies, **12**, **17**, **47**, **107–148**. *See
   also* groups
administrative templates, **108–109**,
   121, **123–124**, *124*, **127**
application deployment, **131–148**
   Add/Remove Programs Control
     Panel and, 133, 136, 140,
     146
   application assignment scripts
     (.AAS), 134, 146
   assigning applications to users and
     computers, 135, 144–145,
     146
   configuring application deploy-
     ment settings, 136–140, *137*,
     139, *140*
   creating application categories,
     139–140, *140*, 142, 146
   creating directory shares for, 134–
     135, 144
   defined, **131**
   deleting software packages from
     Group Policy Objects, 140–
     141, *141*
   exam essentials, **145–146**
   exercises, **143–145**
   file extension mappings, 138, *139*
   initialization files (.ZAP), 133,
     146
   logging, 142
   optimizing, 142–143
   package default settings, 137–
     138, *137*
   patches (.MSP files), 133, 146
   preparing for, 134–135
   publishing applications, 136,
     144–145, 146
   sample questions, **147–148**
   Software Installation Properties
     dialog box, 136–140, *137*,
     139, *140*
   terms and concepts defined, **146–
     147**

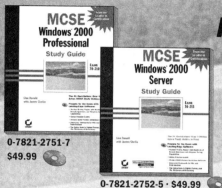

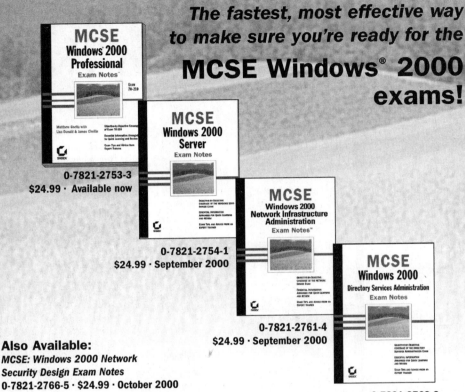